P9-EEB-063

More Praise for

FEEL THE FEAR . . . AND
DO IT ANYWAY

"It's a must! The most practical guide to personal empower-
ment I have ever read. *Feel the Fear . . . and Do It Anyway*
goes to number one on my recommended reading list."
—Jordan Paul, coauthor of *Do I Have to
Give Up on Me to Be Loved By You?*

"[A book that] calls to the courageous soul in each of us—
to which the soul answers 'Yes!' so clearly we cannot help
but hear."   —Gini Kopecky, *Redbook*

"Comforting, practical, upbeat . . . A commonsense exercise program for the mind."   —*The San Diego Union*

"Unlike most books that purport to help the reader face
life's problems, Susan Jeffers's is full of advice that is
actually workable. Moreover, it's a pleasure to read."
—*McCall's*

"Sage, commonsense advice. Useful for its encouragement
and insights."   —*Booklist*

"Unique . . . A truly revolutionary tool to fearless living!"
—*The Pilot*

*I'm Okay . . . You're a Brat: Setting the Priorities
and Freeing You from the Guilt and Mad Myths
of Parenthood**

Life Is Huge!: Laughing, Loving, and Learning from It All

The Little Book of Confidence

The Little Book of Peace of Mind

*Losing a Love and Finding a Life: Healing the
Pain of a Broken Relationship*

*Opening Our Hearts to Men: Taking Charge of Our
Lives and Creating a Love That Works**

Thoughts of Power and Love*

Audiotapes and CDs from Live Appearances

The Art of Fearbusting

A Fearbusting Workshop

Flirting from the Heart

Opening Our Hearts to Each Other

Feel the Fear . . . and Do It Anyway®

Dynamic Techniques for Turning
Fear, Indecision, and Anger into
Power, Action, and Love

Susan Jeffers, PhD

HARVEST
An Imprint of WILLIAM MORROW

FEEL THE FEAR . . . AND DO IT ANYWAY. Copyright © 1987, 2007 by Susan Jeffers, PhD. Copyright © 2023 by the Jeffers/ Shelmerdine Family Trust. All rights reserved. Printed in the United States of America. No part of this book may be used or reproduced in any manner whatsoever without written permission except in the case of brief quotations embodied in critical articles and reviews. For information, address HarperCollins Publishers, 195 Broadway, New York, NY 10007.

HarperCollins books may be purchased for educational, business, or sales promotional use. For information, please email the Special Markets Department at SPsales@harpercollins.com.

Originally published in the United States in 1987 by Harcourt Brace Jovanovich, Inc.

20th Anniversary Edition published in the United States in 2007 by Ballantine Books.

Feel the Fear . . . and Do It Anyway is a registered trademark of the Jeffers/Shelmerdine Family Trust.

ISBN 978-0-06-329129-4

22 23 24 25 26 LBC 5 4 3 2 1

For the wonderful gifts of life and love, I dedicate this book to the loving memory of my mother, Jeanne, and my father, Leon.

I also dedicate this book to my jewel of a husband, Mark Shelmerdine, who brings so much love and joy into my life. I am truly blessed.

Contents

INTRODUCTION

Opening the Door

What is it for you?

Fear of . . .
public speaking
asserting yourself
making decisions
intimacy
becoming a parent
not becoming a parent
changing jobs
being alone
being with people
aging
driving
following your dream
losing a loved one
ending a relationship?

Is it some of the above? All of the above? Perhaps you could add a few more to the list. Never mind . . . join the crowd! Fear seems to be epidemic in our society. We fear beginnings; we fear endings. We fear changing; we fear "staying stuck." We fear success; we fear failure. We fear living; we fear dying.

Whatever the fear, this book will give you the insight and tools to vastly improve your ability to handle any given situation. You will move from a place of pain, paralysis, and depression (feelings that often accompany fear) to one of power, energy, and excitement.

You may be surprised and encouraged to learn that while inability to deal with fear may look and feel like a psychological problem, in most cases it isn't. I believe it is primarily an educational problem, and that by reeducating the mind, you can accept fear as simply a fact of life rather than a barrier to success. (This should be a relief to all of you out there who have been wondering, "What's wrong with me?")

My conviction that fear can be dealt with through reeducation came about through my own experiences. When I was younger, I was always run by fear, so it wasn't surprising that for years I hung on to many things in my life that clearly were not working for me.

Part of my problem was the nonstop little voice inside my head that kept telling me, "YOU'D BETTER NOT CHANGE YOUR SITUATION. THERE'S NOTHING ELSE OUT THERE FOR YOU. YOU'LL NEVER MAKE IT ON YOUR OWN." You know the voice I'm talking about—the one that keeps reminding you, "DON'T TAKE A CHANCE, YOU MIGHT MAKE A MISTAKE. BOY, WILL YOU BE SORRY!"

My fear never seemed to abate, and I didn't have a moment's peace. Even my doctorate in psychology didn't seem to do me much good. Then one day, as I was dressing for work, I reached the turning point. I happened to glance in the mirror, and I saw an all-too-familiar sight—eyes red and puffy from tears of self-pity. Suddenly rage welled up inside me, and I began shouting at my reflection, "ENOUGH . . . ENOUGH . . . ENOUGH!" I shouted until I had no more energy (or voice) left.

When I stopped, I felt a strange and wonderful sense of relief and calm I had never felt before. Without realizing it at the time, I had gotten in touch with a very powerful part of myself that before that moment I hadn't even known existed. I took another long look in the mirror and smiled as I nodded my head YES . . . YES! The old familiar voice of doom and gloom was drowned out, at least temporarily, and a new voice had come to the fore—one that spoke of strength and love and joy and all good things. At that moment I knew I was not going to let fear get the best of me. I would find a way to rid myself of the negativism that prevailed in my life. Thus, my odyssey began.

An ancient sage once said, "When the student is ready, the teacher will appear." The student was ready, and teachers appeared from all over the place. I began to read, attend workshops, and talk to as many people as would listen. Diligently following every suggestion and lead, I *unlearned* the thinking that had been keeping me a prisoner of my own insecurities. I began to see the world as a less threatening and more joyous place; I started to see myself as someone who had purpose; and I experienced the meaning of love for the first time in my life.

At this point I began to notice many other people struggling with the same barriers I had finally learned to push through— the main barrier being fear. How could I help them? Realizing that the processes that had transformed my life were educational in nature, I was convinced that the same techniques I had used could be taught to anyone, regardless of age, gender, or background. I was able to test my theory in the real world by teaching a course at the New School, in New York City. Called "Feel the Fear . . . and Do It Anyway," the course was described as follows:

> *Whenever we take a chance and enter unfamiliar territory or put ourselves into the world in a new way, we experience fear. Very often this fear keeps us from moving ahead with our lives. The trick is to* FEEL THE FEAR AND DO IT ANYWAY. *Together we will explore the barriers that keep us from experiencing life the way we want to live it. So many of us short-circuit our living by choosing the path that is the most comfortable. Through readings, class discussions, and interesting exercises we will learn to identify our excuses for "staying stuck" and develop the techniques for taking control of our own lives.*

My experiment with taking the concept of fear out of the realm of therapy and placing it in the area of education was extremely successful. My students were amazed at how shifting their thinking magically reshaped their lives. The concepts worked for them as they had worked for me. And, not surprisingly, my students also became my teachers. They reaffirmed and added to my fund of knowledge as I listened carefully to their wisdom.

Those of you who are reading this book have acknowledged

that wherever you are in life at this moment is not exactly the place you want to be. Something needs changing, and until now you haven't been able to take the steps to change it. By reading these words, I know that whatever your circumstances, you are ready to start taking charge of your life.

I'm not promising that change is easy. It takes courage to mold your life the way you want it to be. There are all sorts of real and imagined obstacles that get in the way. They need not deter you. In your journey through this book you will become familiar with many concepts, exercises, and other devices to help you unravel the complexities of fear . . . and thus help you deal with it. You will learn:

how it can be impossible to make a mistake or a wrong decision
how to let go of negative programming
how it is impossible to be taken advantage of
how to say yes to all circumstances in your life
how to raise your level of self-esteem
how to become more mindful
how to become more assertive
how to connect with the powerhouse within
how to create more love, trust, and satisfaction
how to deal with resistance from significant others as you take more control of your life
how to experience more enjoyment
how to make your dreams become a reality
how to see yourself as having purpose and meaning.

As you read the book, in whichever format you choose, high-light or underline those sections of the book that "speak" to you, so that later you can easily find critical passages to help you face new situations in life. It takes a lot of reinforcement to incorporate new concepts into your behavior, so commit yourself to doing the exercises. The amount of improvement you experience will depend on how much you are willing to participate actively. Also, the more you get involved, the more fun you will have. You will be surprised and pleased at the amount of satisfaction that comes as you take each little step forward.

No matter what degree of insecurity you are feeling, a part of you knows there is a lot of wonderful "stuff" within you just waiting to be let out and NOW is the ideal time for opening the door to the power and love within.

handle it I'll handle it I'll handle it I'll handle it I'll handle it I'll handle it I'll handle it I'll handle it I'll handle i
dle it I'll handle it I'll handle it I'll handle it I'll handle it I'll handle it I'll handle it I'll handle it I'll handle it I'll
handle it I'll handle it I'll handle it I'll handle it I'll handle it I'll handle it I'll handle it I'll handle it I'll handle i
dle it I'll handle it I'll handle it I'll handle it I'll handle it I'll handle it I'll handle it I'll handle it I'll handle it I'll
handle it I'll handle it I'll handle it I'll handle it I'll handle it I'll handle it I'll handle it I'll handle it I'll handle i
dle it I'll handle it I'll handle it I'll handle it I'll handle it I'll handle it I'll handle it I'll handle it I'll handle it I'll
handle it I'll handle it I'll handle it I'll handle it I'll handle it I'll handle it I'll handle it I'll handle it I'll handle
dle it I'll handle it I'll handle it I'll handle it I'll handle it I'll handle it I'll handle it I'll handle it I'll handle it I'll
handle it I'll handle it I'll handle it I'll handle it I'll handle it I'll handle it I'll handle it I'll handle it I'll handle i
dle it I'll handle it I'll handle it I'll handle it I'll handle it I'll handle it I'll handle it I'll handle it I'll handle it I'll
handle it I'll handle i
dle it I'll handle it I'll I
handle it I'll handle i
dle it I'll handle it I'll I
handle it I'll handle i
dle it I'll handle it I'll I
handle it I'll handle i
dle it I'll handle it I'll I
handle it I'll handle i
dle it I'll handle it I'll I
handle it I'll handle i
dle it I'll handle it I'll I
handle it I'll handle i
dle it I'll handle it I'll I
handle it I'll handle i

1.

What Are You Afraid of . . . and Why?

'll handle it I'll handle i
ndle it I'll handle it I'll I
'll handle it I'll handle i
ndle it I'll handle it I'll I
'll handle it I'll handle i
ndle it I'll handle it I'll I
'll handle it I'll handle i
ndle it I'll handle it I'll I
'll handle it I'll handle i
ndle it I'll handle it I'll I
'll handle it I'll handle i
ndle it I'll handle it I'll I
'll handle it I'll handle i
ndle it I'll handle it I'll I
'll handle it I'll handle i

dle it I'll handle it I'll handle it I'll handle it I'll handle it I'll handle it I'll handle it I'll handle it I'll handle it I'll
handle it I'll handle it I'll handle it I'll handle it I'll handle it I'll handle it I'll handle it I'll handle it I'll handle
dle it I'll handle it I'll handle it I'll handle it I'll handle it I'll handle it I'll handle it I'll handle it I'll handle it I'll
handle it I'll handle it I'll handle it I'll handle it I'll handle it I'll handle it I'll handle it I'll handle it I'll handle i
dle it I'll handle it I'll handle it I'll handle it I'll handle it I'll handle it I'll handle it I'll handle it I'll handle it I'll
handle it I'll handle it I'll handle it I'll handle it I'll handle it I'll handle it I'll handle it I'll handle it I'll handle
dle it I'll handle it I'll handle it I'll handle it I'll handle it I'll handle it I'll handle it I'll handle it I'll handle it I'll
handle it I'll handle it I'll handle it I'll handle it I'll handle it I'll handle it I'll handle it I'll handle it I'll handle i
dle it I'll handle it I'll handle it I'll handle it I'll handle it I'll handle it I'll handle it I'll handle it I'll handle it I'll
handle it I'll handle it I'll handle it I'll handle it I'll handle it I'll handle it I'll handle it I'll handle it I'll handle
dle it I'll handle it I'll handle it I'll handle it I'll handle it I'll handle it I'll handle it I'll handle it I'll handle it I'll
handle it I'll handle it I'll handle it I'll handle it I'll handle it I'll handle it I'll handle it I'll handle it I'll handle i
dle it I'll handle it I'll handle it I'll handle it I'll handle it I'll handle it I'll handle it I'll handle it I'll handle it I'll
handle it I'll handle it I'll handle it I'll handle it I'll handle it I'll handle it I'll handle it I'll handle it I'll handle
dle it I'll handle it I'll handle it I'll handle it I'll handle it I'll handle it I'll handle it I'll handle it I'll handle it I'll
handle it I'll handle it I'll handle it I'll handle it I'll handle it I'll handle it I'll handle it I'll handle it I'll handle i
dle it I'll handle it I'll handle it I'll handle it I'll handle it I'll handle it I'll handle it I'll handle it I'll handle it I'll

am about to teach another fear class. The classroom is empty. I am waiting for my new group of students to appear. My nervousness about teaching these classes disappeared a long time ago. Not only have I taught it many times, but also I know my students before I meet them. They are like the rest of us: all trying to do the best they can and all uncertain about whether they're good enough. It never varies.

As the students enter the room, I can feel the tension. They sit as far apart from one another as possible, until the seats between must be filled because of lack of space. They don't talk to one another, but sit nervously, expectantly. I love them for their courage to admit that their lives are not working the way they want them to work. And their presence in the class signifies they are ready to do something about it.

I begin by going around the room asking each student to tell the rest of us what they are having difficulty confronting in life. Their stories unfold:

Oliver wants to change his career of 14 years and follow his dreams of becoming an artist.
Emily is an actress who wants to discover why she finds all kinds of excuses for not attending auditions.
Sarah wants to leave a marriage of 15 years.
Ethan wants to get over his fear of aging. He is all of 32.
Jean is a senior who wants to confront her doctor; he treats her like a child and never gives her any straight answers.
Meredith is openly gay, except at work. She is very career-oriented and believes that her sexual orientation would keep her from being promoted because there are no other openly gay employees in her company.

3

Tess wants to expand her business but can't make the
required leap into the next step.

Laurie wants to confront her husband with things that
have been bothering her about his attitude toward her.

Gabe wants to get over a fear of rejection that makes it
very difficult to ask anyone on a date.

Madison wants to know why she is unhappy when she has
everything one could possibly want in life.

Richard is retired and feels useless. He fears his life is
over.

And so it goes until everyone's story is heard.

I'm fascinated with what happens during the go-around. As
each person shares from the heart, the entire atmosphere begins
to change. The tension quickly fades and relief is expressed on
everyone's face. A bond begins to form.

First, my students begin to realize they are not the only ones in
the world feeling afraid. Second, they begin to see how attractive
people become as they open up and share their feelings. Long
before the last person has spoken, a feeling of warmth and cama-
raderie pervades the room. They are strangers no more.

Although the backgrounds and situations of the class members
vary greatly, it does not take long for the surface layers of their
particular stories to disappear, opening the way for everyone to
touch on a very human level. The common denominator is the
fact that fear is keeping all of them from experiencing life the way
they want to experience it.

The scenario above repeats itself in each fear class I teach. At
this point you might be wondering how one course can accom-
modate all the diverse fears reported by the class members—
their needs seem to be so varied. It's true. They do seem varied
until we dig a little deeper and look at the underlying cause of all
their fears—and everyone else's.

Fear can be broken down into three levels. The first level is
the surface story, such as the ones described above. This level of
fear can be divided into two types: those that "happen" and those
that require action. Here is a partial list of Level 1 fears divided
into these types:

LEVEL 1 FEARS

Those That "Happen"	*Those Requiring Action*
Aging	Making decisions
Becoming disabled	Going back to school
Retirement	Changing a career
Being alone	Making friends
Children leaving home	Ending or beginning
Natural disasters	a relationship
Loss of financial security	Having a child
Dying	Asserting oneself
War	Traveling
Illness	Being interviewed
Losing a loved one	Driving
Accidents	Public speaking
Rape	Making a mistake
Bankruptcy	Intimacy

You might have a few you can add to the list. As I hinted earlier, you wouldn't be alone if you said to yourself, "Some of the above" or even "All of the above." There is a reason for this. One of the insidious qualities of fear is that it tends to permeate many areas of our lives. For example, if you fear making new friends, it then stands to reason you also may fear going to parties, having intimate relationships, applying for jobs, and so on.

This is made clearer by a look at the second layer of fear, which has a very different feel from that of Level 1. Level 2 fears are not situation-oriented; they involve the ego.

LEVEL 2 FEARS

Rejection	Being hustled
Success	Helplessness
Failure	Disapproval
Feeling shame	Disappointment
Being vulnerable	Loss of image

Level 2 fears have to do with inner states of mind rather than exterior situations. They reflect your sense of self and your ability to handle this world. This explains why generalized fear takes place. If you are afraid of being rejected, this fear will affect almost every area of your life. Rejection is rejection—wherever it is found. So you begin to protect yourself, and, as a result, greatly limit yourself. You begin to shut down and close out the world around you. Look over the Level 2 list once again, and you will see how any one of these fears can greatly impact many areas of your life.

Level 3 gets down to the nitty-gritty of the issue: the biggest fear of all—the one that really keeps you stuck. Are you ready?

LEVEL 3 FEAR

I can't handle it!

"That's it? That's the big deal?" you may ask. I know you're disappointed and wanted something much more dramatic than that. But the truth is this:

At the bottom of every one of your fears is simply the fear that you can't handle whatever life may bring you.

Let's test this. The Level 1 fears translate to:

I can't handle illness.
I can't handle making a mistake.
I can't handle losing my job.
I can't handle getting old.
I can't handle being alone.
I can't handle making a fool out of myself.
I can't handle not getting the job.
I can't handle losing my partner.
I can't handle losing my money . . . etc.

The Level 2 fears translate to:

I can't handle the responsibilities of success.
I can't handle failure.
I can't handle being rejected . . . etc.

Thus Level 3—simply, "I can't handle it!"
The truth is:

• • •

If you knew you could handle anything that came your way, what would you possibly have to fear?

• • •

The answer is: NOTHING!

I know you are probably not jumping up and down for joy just yet, but believe me when I tell you I have just given you a great piece of news. What I have just told you means you can handle all your fears without having to control anything in the outside world. This should be a tremendous relief. You no longer have to control what your partner does, what your friends do, what your children do, or what your boss does. You don't have to control what happens at an interview, what happens at your job, what happens in your new career, what happens to your money, or what happens in the stock market.

• • •

All you have to do to diminish your fear is to develop more trust in your ability to handle whatever comes your way!

• • •

I am belaboring the point because it is so critical. From this moment on, every time you feel afraid, remind yourself that it is simply because you are not feeling good enough about yourself. Then proceed to use one or more of the tools in this book to help build yourself up. You have your task clearly mapped out for you. There is no reason for confusion.

I've often been asked to explain why we have so little trust in ourselves. I don't really know the answer to that. I know that some fear is instinctual and healthy and keeps us alert to trouble. The rest—the part that holds us back from personal growth—is inappropriate and destructive, and perhaps can be blamed on our conditioning.

In all my life I have never heard a mother call out to her child as he or she goes off to school, "Take a lot of risks today, darling." She is more likely to convey to her child, "Be careful, darling." This "Be careful" carries with it a double message: "The world is really dangerous out there" . . . *and* . . . "You won't be able to handle it." What Mom is really saying, of course, is "If something happens to you, I won't be able to handle it." You see, she is only passing on her lack of trust in *her* ability to handle what comes her way.

I can remember wanting desperately to have a two-wheel bicycle and my mother's refusal to buy me one. Her answer to my pleas was always the same: "I love you too much. I don't want anything to happen to you." I translated this to mean "You are not competent enough to handle a two-wheel bike." Having become older and wiser, I realize now that she was really saying: "If anything happens to you, I will fall apart."

This overprotective mother of mine was once in intensive care after serious surgery, with tubes down her nose and her throat. When I was told it was time for me to leave, I whispered in her ear—not knowing if she could hear me—that I loved her and would be back later. As I was walking toward the door, I heard a small, weak voice behind me saying—you guessed it—"Be careful." Even in her anesthetic stupor, she was sending me admonitions of doom and gloom. And I know she typifies the great percentage of parents out there. Considering how many "be carefuls" our parents bombarded us with, it is amazing we even managed to walk out the front door!

Apart from such seemingly obvious connections, the cause of our fear quite possibly lies elsewhere. But does it really matter where our self-doubts come from? I believe not. It is not my approach to analyze the whys and wherefores of troublesome areas of the mind. It is often impossible to figure out what the actual causes of negative patterns are, and even if we did know, the knowing doesn't necessarily change them. I believe that if something is troubling you, simply start from where you are and take the action necessary to change it.

In this case, you know that you don't like the fact that lack of trust in yourself is stopping you from getting what you want out of life. Knowing this creates a very clear, even laserlike, focus on what needs to be changed. You don't have to scatter your energy wondering why. It doesn't matter. What matters is that you begin now to develop your trust in yourself, until you reach the point where you will be able to say:

· · ·

Whatever happens to me, given any situation, I can handle it!

· · ·

I can hear the doubters out there saying, "Oh, come on now, how do you handle paralysis, or the death of a child, or cancer?" I understand your skepticism. Remember that I was once a doubter myself. Just read on and let the book unfold. Give yourself a winning chance by using the tools provided throughout this book. As you do, you will find yourself coming closer and closer to such a high level of self-confidence that you will ultimately begin to realize that you can handle anything that comes your way. Never let these three little words out of your mind—possibly the most important three little words you'll ever hear:

· · ·

I'll handle it!

· · ·

2.

Can't You Make It Go Away?

Morgan's still waiting for the fear to go away. She had always planned to return to college once her children were in school, but she now notices it's been four years since her youngest child entered first grade. New excuses have popped up since that time: "I want to be here when the children come home from school"; "We really don't have the money"; "My husband will feel neglected."

Although it is true that certain logistics would have to be worked out, that is not the reason for her hesitation. In fact, her husband is willing to help her in any way he can. He is concerned about her restlessness, and often encourages her to fulfill her life-long dream of becoming a fashion designer.

Each time Morgan thinks about signing up for classes at her local college, something stops her. "When I'm not so frightened, then I'll do it"; "When I feel a little better about myself, then I'll do it." Most likely Morgan is going to wait a very long time.

The problem is that her thinking is all mixed up. The logic she uses automatically programs her for failure. She will never break the fear barrier until she is made aware of her faulty thinking; she simply does not "see" what is obvious to those who are out there doing it.

Nor did I until I was forced to. Before my divorce from my first husband, I was rather like a child, allowing him to take over the practicalities of my life. After my divorce, I had no choice but to start doing things on my own. Small things, such as fixing the vacuum cleaner all by myself, brought me enormous satisfaction. Learning to eat in a restaurant alone was awkward but ultimately pleasant. The first night I invited people to my home for dinner as a single person was a monumental leap. The day I booked tickets for my first trip by myself was a day for celebration.

As I began to *do* things on my own, I began to taste the deliciousness of an emerging self-confidence. It wasn't all comfortable—in fact, a lot of it was extremely uncomfortable. I felt like a child learning to walk and falling frequently. But with each step, I felt a little surer of my ability to handle my life.

As my confidence grew, I kept waiting for the fear to go away. Yet each time I ventured out into a new territory, I felt frightened and unsure of myself. "Well," I told myself, "just keep putting yourself out there. Eventually the fear will go away." It never did! One day a light bulb went on in my head as I suddenly realized the following "truth":

TRUTH 1

The fear will never go away as long as I continue to grow.

As long as I continued to push out into the world, as long as I continued to stretch my capabilities, as long as I continued to take new risks in making my dreams come true, I was going to experience fear. What a revelation! Like Morgan, and so many of you reading this book, I had grown up waiting for the fear to go away before I took any chances. "When I am no longer afraid . . . then!" For most of my life, I had played the WHEN/THEN game. And it never worked.

Once again, you are probably not jumping up and down with joy. I am aware that this revelation is not exactly one you wanted to hear. If you are like the students in my classes, you were hoping that my words of wisdom would miraculously make your fears go away. I'm sorry to say it doesn't work that way. On the other hand, rather than thinking of it as a disappointment, consider it a relief that you no longer have to work so hard on getting rid of the fear. It isn't going to go away! Not to worry. As you build confidence in yourself with the exercises suggested herein, your relationship with fear will dramatically alter.

Not long after discovering Truth 1, I made another important discovery that contributed enormously to my growth:

TRUTH 2

The only way to get rid of the fear of doing something is to go out and do it.

This sounds contradictory to Truth 1, yet it isn't. Fear of *particular* situations dissolved when I finally confronted them. The "doing it" comes before the fear goes away.

I can illustrate this by recounting my first teaching experience when I was studying for my doctorate. I was not much older than my students and I was teaching a subject in which I had dubious expertise—the psychology of aging. I anticipated the first class period with a tremendous sense of dread. During the three days prior to the class, my stomach felt like it was on a roller-coaster. I had prepared eight hours of work for a one-hour class. I had handwritten enough material for three lectures. None of this took away my fear. When the first day of class finally arrived, I felt like I was being sent to the guillotine. As I stood in front of my students, I could feel my heart pounding and my knees shaking. Somehow I got through that class period, but I was not ecstatically looking forward to the second one the following week.

Thankfully, things were easier the next time. (If not, I might have left teaching permanently!) I started to become familiar with the faces in the classroom and connected some of the names to the faces. The third class was better than the second, as I started to relax and go with the flow of the students. By our sixth session, I was actually looking forward to standing in front of my class. The interaction with my students was stimulating and challenging. One day, as I was approaching that once-dreaded classroom, I realized I was no longer afraid. My fear had turned into sweet anticipation.

I had to teach a number of different courses before I was comfortable walking into a class without voluminous notes. But there did come a day when all I had in my hand was a one-page outline of what I intended to cover that period. I realized how far I had come. I had felt the fear . . . and done it anyway. As a result, I got rid of my fear of teaching. Yet, when I took my teaching into a broader arena and actually appeared on television, once again I experienced fear, until my "doing it" often enough eliminated my fear of that as well. And so it goes.

Another part of the WHEN/THEN game I used to play had to do with self-esteem. "When I feel better about myself . . . then I'll do it." This is another mix-up in the order of reality. I kept thinking that if I could improve my self-image, then the fear would go away and I could start accomplishing things. I didn't know exactly *how* my self-image was going to improve. Perhaps by my growing older and wiser, or through feedback from other people, or a miracle would make me feel wonderful about myself. I actually bought myself a belt buckle that read I'M TERRIFIC, thinking that through osmosis I'd get the message.

Maybe all those things did help a little. What really made the difference, however, was the sense of accomplishment I felt in pushing through fear and doing things on my own. Finally, this became clear:

TRUTH 3

The only way to feel better about myself is to go out . . . and do it.

The "doing it" comes *before* the feeling better about yourself. When you make something happen, not only does the fear of the situation go away, but also you get a big bonus: you do a lot toward building your self-confidence. It's fairly predictable, however, that when you've finally mastered something and gotten rid of the fear, you will decide there is something else out there you want to accomplish, and—guess what! The fear begins again as you prepare to meet a new challenge.

Through all the workshops and seminars I attended in my

early stages of dealing with fear, I was relieved to learn something else that made me feel infinitely better about myself:

TRUTH 4

Not only am I going to experience fear whenever I'm on unfamiliar territory, but so is everyone else.

I said to myself: *"You mean all those people out there that I've been envying because they're not afraid to move ahead with their lives have really been afraid? Why didn't somebody tell me!?"* I guess I never asked. I was sure I was the only person out there feeling so inadequate. It was such a relief to realize I was not alone in this. I had the rest of the world to keep me company.

A great example of this is the prolific TV producer, creator, and writer Shonda Rhimes. She's known internationally for her shows *Grey's Anatomy, Scandal,* and *How to Get Away with Murder.* Despite being hugely successful, she hated being in the spotlight. She's an introvert and found that the glamorous Hollywood life— large events, parties, and award shows—caused her severe anxiety. So she never said yes to invitations. When her older sister pointed this out to her, Shonda decided to turn her life around. She vowed to say yes for a year, no matter what. Her decision became the basis of her bestselling book, *Year of Yes,* which chronicles how she overcame her intense fear of putting herself in the spotlight.

If you are aware of the Fear Truths, Shonda's fear will not come as a surprise. Writing is a behind-the-scenes occupation—no wonder Hollywood parties made her nervous. Being the center of attention is something that she's not comfortable with, so of course she would be scared. After her Year of Yes, Shonda found that stretching past her boundaries increased both her self-worth and her self-confidence. Simply put, that is the way it works—for all of us. By virtue of our being human, we share the same feelings. Fear is no exception.

There are many stories similar to Shonda Rhimes's experience.

Until you are in touch with the Fear Truths, you will hear about and read and see these stories and not notice the underlying principles operating in them. You may never relate the experiences of others, especially celebrities, to your own life. You may think they are lucky because they aren't afraid to put themselves out there. Not so! They had to push through a tremendous amount of fear to get where they are today . . . and they are still pushing.

Those who have successfully dealt with fear all their lives seem to have known, consciously or unconsciously, the message in this book: you must feel the fear . . . and do it anyway. A very successful friend of mine, a self-made man who allowed nothing to stop him along the way, pondered the title of my course one day, nodded, and said, "Yes, I guess that is the way I've always lived my life, without consciously realizing that's what I've been doing. I can't remember not being afraid, but it never occurred to me that fear would prevent me from taking the risks necessary to get what I wanted. I just went ahead and did what I had to do to make my ideas work—despite the fear."

There are so many inspiring examples of people becoming hugely successful even after experiencing daunting setbacks. Bill Gates's first company failed; later he founded Microsoft. Oprah Winfrey was fired from her first broadcast news job. The basketball legend Michael Jordan was cut from his high school basketball team. The first book by Stephen King, the author of more than 100 books, was rejected more than 30 times.

Pushing through the fear is not just for the wildly successful. I know a woman who divorced in her late 30s, when she set out to find a job, wanting to pursue a career in law enforcement. She became a police officer at the age of 39, at a time when there were few women police officers. If you think she didn't have any fear, you would be very wrong.

These are just a few examples of how people have consciously or unconsciously felt their fear and moved past it. Feeling fear is very lonely, but it helps to know that we all experience it.

If you have not been successful in dealing with fear, you probably never learned the Fear Truths, and so you interpreted fear as a signal to retreat rather than as a green light to move ahead. You have tended to play those WHEN/THEN games I mentioned earlier. All you have to do to find a way out of your self-imposed prison is to retrain your thinking.

RETRAIN YOUR THINKING

A first step in retraining your thinking is to say the Fear Truths at least ten times a day for the next month. As you will shortly discover, retraining faulty thinking takes constant repetition. *Knowing* the Fear Truths is not enough. You have to keep feeding them to yourself until they become a part of your being—until you start to reverse your behavior and move *toward* your desired goals, rather than retreat. There will be more later about why repetition is so important. For now, just trust me and repeat the Fear Truths over and over again.

Before you begin, however, I'd like to add one very important Fear Truth to the list. You might already have been asking yourself, "Why should I put myself through all the discomfort that comes with taking risks? Why don't I just go on living my life the way I've been living it?" You might find my answer to that question surprising:

TRUTH 5

Pushing through fear is less frightening
than living with the underlying fear that
comes from a feeling of helplessness.

Read it again. I know it's hard to take in at first. It means that no matter how "secure" any of us feel in the little cocoon we have built for ourselves, we live, consciously or unconsciously, with the fear that the day of reckoning will eventually come.

The more helpless we feel, the more severe is the undercurrent of dread that comes with knowing there are situations in life over which we have no control—such as the death of a spouse or the loss of a job. We find ourselves becoming obsessive about possible catastrophes: "What if . . . ?" Fear permeates our lives. That is the irony of Truth 5: people who refuse to take risks live with a feeling of dread that is far more severe than what they would feel if they took the risks necessary to make them less helpless—only they don't know it!

I can illustrate this with the case of Janice, a woman who "planned" her life in such a way as to avoid risk-taking as much as possible. She married a successful businessman who handled both their lives. Janice allowed this situation because it was more comfortable for her never to put herself on the line. But, as the saying goes, "Life is what happens when we've made other plans!" At the age of 53, her husband, Dick, had a stroke, which left him partially disabled. One day she was totally *taken* care of and the next she was totally *taking* care of.

The transition wasn't easy. After fighting the rage of "Why did this happen to me?" she started to accept the fact that she was now in charge of both her own and her husband's survival. Numbed, she went through the motions of learning his business, handling decisions regarding his health, and waking up every morning with the understanding that it was now up to her. After a while, the numbness left, the fog cleared, and she discovered a profound sense of peace she had never experienced before. She started to realize the heavy price she had paid to be taken care of.

Prior to her husband's stroke, Janice's thinking had been permeated with the phrase "what if." She always worried about the future, never enjoying her todays. She had lived with an underlying dread: "My God, what if something happened to him?" She had often remarked to her friends, "I hope I die before he does. I couldn't live without him." And she thought she couldn't—which is a less than satisfactory way to go through life. This all changed as she found strength she never thought she had. She now knows the answer to her "what if" question. The answer is "I'll handle it!"

Janice had never realized she was living with terror all her life until that terror disappeared. The new fears were nothing compared to her old fears about survival. Her husband recovered enough for them to live a satisfying life together. He, too, faced one of his biggest fears—becoming disabled. He got the answer to his "what if" question, which was also "I'll handle it." They both handled it beautifully. In fact, through this experience they learned the real meaning of love.

By now you've gotten the picture. We can't escape fear. We can only transform it into a companion that accompanies us in all our exciting adventures; it is not an anchor holding us transfixed in one spot. Some people have told me they are never afraid, but when I question them, they reveal that we are just differing on semantics. Yes, they feel nervous or anxious sometimes—they simply never labeled it fear.

As far as I know, everyone feels fear as they move forward through life. It is absolutely possible that there are some evolved souls in this world who never experience fear and I have not met them. If I do, I promise I will become their avid student and report back to you with their secrets. You see, I "know" on some deep level there is nothing to fear. It's the surface level that needs convincing. In the meantime, I've learned to "feel the fear . . . and do it anyway!" As I do, whether I feel the fear or not becomes irrelevant. My life will work in either case . . . as will yours.

FIVE TRUTHS ABOUT FEAR

1. The fear will never go away as long as I continue to grow.

2. The only way to get rid of the fear of doing something is to go out . . . and do it.

3. The only way to feel better about myself is to go out . . . and do it.

4. Not only am I going to experience fear whenever I'm on unfamiliar territory, but so is everyone else.

5. Pushing through fear is less frightening than living with the underlying fear that comes from a feeling of helplessness.

3.

From Pain
to Power

I am powerful and I am loving! I am powerful and I am loving!

The last chapter revealed a critical insight indeed, and that is:

If everybody feels fear when approaching something totally new in life, yet so many are out there "doing it" despite the fear, then we must conclude that **fear is not the problem.**

Obviously, the real issue has nothing to do with the fear itself, but rather, how we *hold* the fear. For some, the fear is totally irrelevant. For others, it creates a state of paralysis. The former hold their fear from a position of power (choice, energy, and action), and the latter hold it from a position of pain (helplessness, depression, and paralysis).

The chart below illustrates this concept.

How We Hold Fear

Pain	Power
Helplessness	Choice
Depression	Energy
Paralysis	Action

From this it can be seen that the secret in handling fear is to move yourself from a position of pain to a position of power. The fact that you have the fear then becomes irrelevant.

Let's talk about the word "power." Some people say that they do not like the concept of power and want no part of it. It is true that in our world the word "power" has some negative overtones. It often implies control over others and, unfortunately, is often misused.

The kind of power I am talking about is entirely different. In fact, it makes you *less* manipulative of those around you, and certainly more loving. I am talking about *power within the self.* This means power over your perceptions of the world, power over how you react to situations in your life, power to do what is necessary for your own self-growth, power to create joy and satisfaction in your life, power to act, and power to love.

This kind of power has nothing to do with anyone else. It is not egomania, but a healthy self-love. In fact, egomaniacs have absolutely no feeling of power—thus their compelling need to control those around them. Their lack of power leaves them perpetually in a state of fear, since their survival depends on the outside world. No one is more unloving than a person who can't own their own power. Such people spend their lives trying to pull it out of everyone else. Their need creates all sorts of manipulative behavior.

The kind of power I'm talking about leaves you free, since you don't expect the rest of the world to fill you up. It's not the ability to get someone else to do what you want them to do. It's the ability to get yourself to do what you want to do. If you do not own this kind of power, you lose your sense of peace. You are in a very vulnerable place.

I have found that some women are more put off than men are by the concept of power, for obvious reasons. Traditionally, men have been conditioned to believe that to be powerful is good. Although the culture of women and power is changing both globally and at home, sadly, many women are still being conditioned to believe that to be powerful is unfeminine and unattractive. In my experience, nothing could be farther from the truth.

A self-assured woman who is in control of her life draws like a magnet. She is so filled with positive energy that people want to be around her. Yet it is only when she has become powerful within herself that she can become authentic and loving to those around her. The truth is that love and power go together. With power, one can really begin to open up the heart. With no power, love is distorted. People can overcome feeling powerless by learning to trust themselves and tap into inner resources they didn't realize existed.

For anyone reading this book, a good antidote to any inner conflict about power is to repeat the following statements to yourself at least 25 times each morning, noon, and night:

I am powerful and I am loved.

And:

I am powerful and I am loving.

An energizing variation is:

I am powerful and I love it!

Say these three statements aloud right now. Feel the energy the words convey. Their constant repetition will help make the concepts of power and love more compatible and certainly more comfortable.

Now that I've explained the kind of power I'm talking about, let's explore how to use the Pain-to-Power concept in daily life.

The first step is to create a Pain-to-Power Chart, as follows:

Pain-to-Power Chart

Pain ▸ ▸ ▸ ▸ ▸ ▸ ▸ **Power**

As we look at the Pain-to-Power continuum, most of us can place ourselves somewhere in the middle of the chart. We're not totally incapacitated by our fears, but we're not exactly feeling a great sense of power and excitement, nor are we quickly sprinting toward our goals. We seem to be taking the arduous route over the mountain, carrying two suitcases and a watermelon rather than flying on the wings of eagles. As an ancient sage once said, "The pathway is smooth. Why do you throw rocks before you?"

Using the Pain-to-Power Chart as a frame of reference, you can begin to clear out the rocks in front of you. The following steps will help in the clearing process:

CLEARING THE PATH FROM PAIN TO POWER

1. Draw an enlargement of the Pain-to-Power Chart and place it on your wall. Just the simple act of making the enlargement will make you feel a little more powerful. You are already taking action! I recommend creating a chart on paper, but you can also create a graphic on your computer or pad to post on your desktop or on the front page of your phone. The chart is a visual reminder that you are working toward a new, more powerful way of being, so put it in a place where you will see it often.

Remember that much of the trick of moving from pain to power is taking action; ACTION IS VERY POWERFUL! Your chart will serve as a constant reminder of where you want to go in life—from pain to power. *Awareness* is half the battle. Having the chart physically present will also help you motivate yourself to keep moving in the right direction.

2. Just to keep you from taking yourself too seriously, you might want to write somewhere on your chart "Angels fly because they take themselves lightly." I heard this quote by the writer G. K. Chesterton a long time ago, and it still makes me smile. It constantly reminds me that you can drop an awful lot of excess baggage if you learn to play with life instead of fight it.

3. Put a pin at the place on the chart where you see yourself situated at this moment in your life. You can visualize it if you are looking at a screen. Are you in the middle, where you sometimes feel depressed and paralyzed and at other times feel more in control? Or do you definitely find yourself on the far left side, where there is little you are able to do to pull yourself out of the rut? Or perhaps you are already on the right side, where most of the time you feel you are really moving ahead with your life, with only a few areas that need to be worked on. I doubt that anyone reading this book has reached their goal of attaining absolute power over the self. Even the Buddhas have their days! There are always new experiences that challenge a sense of personal power.

4. Each day look at the chart and ask yourself, "Do I see myself at the same place, or have I moved?" Move the pin accordingly.

5. If you keep in mind the direction you want to go in, it will help you make decisions about what you are doing in your life. Before you take any action in life, ask yourself: "Is this action moving me to a more powerful place?" If it isn't, you will think twice about doing it. *A word of caution*: If you go ahead anyway, knowing the action will keep you in a position of pain, don't get angry with yourself. Just notice where you are not taking responsibility. The next time, you can make a different decision. Use your "mistakes" as learning experiences. Remember that each time you get angry at yourself for an action you have taken, you keep yourself on the side of pain.

6. Make your use of the chart fun. Approaching it as a game keeps you light about the situation. If you have children, they can create their own charts, and you can make a family game out of the experience of growing.

7. You might want to make different charts for different areas of your life. To be really powerful, you need to be in charge of all aspects of your life—your work, relationships, environment, body, and so on. Often people are very powerful in some parts of their lives and pathetic in others. For example, I am very powerful in terms of my career but need to work on the area of exercise.

Note that your movement on the chart is determined only by your own intuitive sense of how far you are progressing in gaining more power in your life. No one else can judge that, though they may try. Although your life may look exactly the same to the outside world, it is your own sense of internal peace and growth that determines where you are on the chart. It is, totally, a feeling within.

You may wonder if you really need to go to such lengths to get yourself moving. Trust me—you do! In the beginning, you need all the gimmicks you can get to remind you of where you want to go. You don't become powerful without concentrating on power. As you must have figured out by now, simply knowing what to do does not mean that you do it, or, for that matter, even remember it.

To help you on your Pain-to-Power path, it's important that you begin to develop a Pain-to-Power Vocabulary. The way you use words has a tremendous impact on the quality of your life. Certain words are destructive; others are empowering. Choose to move to a Pain-to-Power Vocabulary as follows:

Pain-to-Power Vocabulary

Pain ▸ ▸ ▸ ▸ ▸ ▸ ▸ Power

I can't	I won't
I should	I could
It's not my fault	I'm totally responsible
It's a problem	It's an opportunity
I'm never satisfied	I want to learn and grow
Life's a struggle	Life's an adventure
I hope	I know
If only	Next time
What will I do?	I know I can handle it
It's terrible	It's a learning experience

The statement "I can't" implies you have no control over your life, whereas "I *won't*" puts a situation in the realm of choice. From this moment on, remove "I can't" from your vocabulary. When you give your subconscious the message "I can't," your subconscious really believes you and registers on its computer: WEAK . . . WEAK . . . WEAK. Your subconscious believes only what it hears, not what is true. You might be saying "I can't" simply to get out of a dinner invitation—such as "I can't come to dinner tonight. I have to prepare for tomorrow's meeting," but your subconscious is registering, "He's weak!" In fact, "I can't come to dinner" is an untruth. The truth is, "I *can* come to dinner, but I *am choosing* to do something that has a higher priority at the moment." But the subconscious can't discern the difference and is still registering "weak."

Although you may want to be more delicate to your host than to utter the above statement, you can still stay away from the words "I can't." "I'd love to come to dinner, but I have a meeting tomorrow that's important to me. I'll feel better walking in totally prepared. So I'll pass for tonight and hope you'll invite me again." That statement has truth, integrity, and power. The subconscious hears you stating your priorities with clarity and choosing the outcome that serves your own growth. Choosing this way doesn't leave you the helpless victim of your meeting.

"I should" is another loser. It, too, implies that you have no choices in life. "*I could*" is more powerful. "I could visit my mother, but I'm choosing to go to the movies today." This puts things in the realm of choice instead of obligation. "I can visit my mother or I can go to the movies. I think I'll choose my mother today." "Shoulds" bring on guilt and upset—totally draining your emotions. It is a passive response to the choices in front of you. Your power is taken away every time you utter the words "I should."

"It's not my fault" is another beauty. Once again, it makes you seem helpless. It's better to take responsibility for whatever happens to you in life than always to be the victim. "It's not my fault I got sick"; "It's not my fault I lost the job." If you are willing to take responsibility, then you might see what you can change in the future. Relative to illness, say, "*I'm totally responsible* for my illness. Let's see what I can do to prevent it from happening again. I can change my diet. I can reduce stress. I can stop smoking. I can get enough sleep." And so on. Watch how powerful you become! The same occurs with the lost job. If you are responsible, you can be better prepared the next time; you can find out what made the difference. You are in control. Each time you find yourself in better control of your life, you are moving to a position of power, which will ultimately reduce your fear level.

"It's a problem" is another deadening phrase. It's heavy and negative. *"It's an opportunity"* opens the door to growth. Each time you can see the gift in life's obstacles, you can handle difficult situations in a rewarding way. Each time you have the opportunity to stretch your capacity to handle the world, the more powerful you become.

"I hope" is another victim's phrase. *"I know"* has far more power.

I hope I will get a job.
I know I will get a job.

What a difference! The first sets you up for worry and sleepless nights. The second has peace and calm about it.

"If only" is boring. You can hear the whine behind it. *"Next time"* implies that you have learned from the situation and will put the learning to use another time. For example, "If only I had signed up for that class" can be restated as "I've learned that space in those classes is limited. Next time, I'll be ready to sign up more quickly."

"There's no way" is a commonly used phrase when we face something daunting. "There's no way I can get there by two o'clock." Using this phrase is like throwing up a roadblock to your actions. It is giving in to defeat before you even start. Why not approach these situations with a *"Let's see what happens"* attitude? Say instead, "Traffic might be heavy, but I'll try to get there by two. Let's just see what happens." See how that feels more powerful? And as a bonus, you will be less stressed knowing that you are doing your best.

"What will I do?" Again you can hear the whine and the fear implied in these words. You, like everyone else, have incredible sources of power within that you haven't used before. It would serve you to say to yourself, *"I know I'll handle it.* I have nothing to worry about." Instead of "I've lost my job! What will I do?" try "I've lost my job. I know I'll handle it."

I've noticed the younger generations use "Really?" as a sort of catch-all word to express skepticism. While there is nothing wrong with skepticism—we should all cultivate a bit of it as part of our critical thinking tool kit—it can become a way of thinking that keeps us disengaged with what's going on around us. Skepticism is a close cousin to cynicism, and both views will put us firmly on the left side of the Pain-to-Power Chart. If we view the world through these dark-tinted glasses we begin to feel numb—not only to the bad things in life, but also to all the wonderful things.

I was in a coffee shop recently, and while waiting for my order to come up, I overheard two young women talking. One of them was telling the other about a friend of hers who was starting her own business selling organic skin-care products. I was shocked when the other young woman responded, "Really? Aren't there enough businesses like that already?" Her friend, who up to that point was excited for her acquaintance, instantly looked deflated. The result of "Really?" was that now both young women had become cynical. Can you imagine how much more uplifting the conversation would have been if the second young woman had replied, "Wow, that's exciting. It's a tough business, but good for her for trying."

"It's terrible" is bandied around in the most inappropriate circumstances. For example, "I lost my wallet. Isn't that terrible?" What's so terrible about losing a wallet? It's certainly an inconvenience; it's hardly terrible. "I gained two pounds. Isn't that terrible?" It's hardly terrible to gain two pounds. Yet that's the way we talk about trivia in our lives. And our subconscious is registering DISASTER . . . DISASTER . . . DISASTER. Replace "It's terrible" with *"It's a learning experience."*

While you might feel more justified in saying "It's terrible" if a loved one has cancer, keep in mind that this attitude takes away your power to deal with the situation. There are many who have learned important things from the experience. I know, because I am one of those people.

My experience of cancer taught me many wonderful things about myself and the people around me. I'd been teaching the spiritual path for years with workshops and seminars and speaking on TV talk shows, so when I discovered I had cancer, I asked myself, "Are you going to say *yes* to this, or are you going to say, 'Why did this happen to me?'" I said *yes* to it, and an enormous amount of expansion emerged from it. Most important, I learned how much I was loved. I saw a tender side of my fiancé, now my husband, that I had never seen before, and our love deepened immeasurably. We stopped taking each other for granted. Also, I changed my life in many positive ways. I became a much more aware eater. I learned how to eliminate the anger, resentment, and stress that were very much a part of my daily life prior to my illness. I allowed myself to become more dependent on my loved ones, softer. I'd been very proud of my independence until that time, but the experience of cancer allowed the gentler parts of me to emerge and enrich my relationships. My cancer experience gave my husband and me an opportunity to contribute something to this world. I wrote a very positive article about my mastectomy, which I know has been of value to many men and women. I learned to face the challenge of cancer and my mastectomy with my sense of humor intact. I chose not to have reconstruction. Now when I have a massage, I tell the masseuse, "I only have one breast, and it's not because you rubbed too hard!" My husband and I appeared on television together to relate our experience, bringing reassurance to viewers. So you see, cancer *can* be a great learning experience and an opportunity to give.

You get the picture. Begin eliminating the "can'ts," "shoulds," "if onlys," "terribles," "no's," and so on from your vocabulary. Maybe these semantic differences seem trivial, but I assure you they are not. Not only does your sense of yourself change with a more powerful vocabulary, but so does your presence in the world. People who display an inner strength are treated differently than those who come across as weak and helpless. The more powerfully you speak, the more you will be a force in the world around you.

As you begin to monitor your vocabulary, you can also bring more power into your life by *expanding your comfort zone*. What does that mean?

Most of us operate within a zone that feels right, and outside of it we are uncomfortable. For example, we might spend $50 for a pair of shoes, but $100 would make us nervous. We might be willing to initiate friendships with people at the office who are at our level in the company, but would be uncomfortable doing so with one of the higher-ups. We might be comfortable hanging out with a few friends we know well, but are reluctant to go to a large New Year's party with more strangers than friends or to a professional convention with colleagues we don't know well. We might go to the local deli when eating alone but would feel really uncomfortable in a luxurious restaurant all by ourself. We might ask for a $5,000 raise, but asking for a $7,000 raise would make us cringe. We may charge $30 an hour for our services, but we don't feel we are worth $35. And so on.

For each one of us that zone of comfort is different, but whether we are aware of it or not, all of us—rich or poor, famous or unknown, gay or straight, male or female or whatever our gender identity—make decisions based on the confines of that comfortable space.

With the current state of technology, it has become easier than ever to stay within our narrowly defined comfort zone. We don't have to visit stores to shop—we can just order online anything our hearts desire, and thereby avoid interacting with salespeople. When a phone call could clear up a question in seconds, how many of us dodge a conversation by sending an email or text? We don't have to meet with people in person when we can talk to them online. For many of us, forgoing personal interactions defines our lifestyle in the 21st century. All these new ways of communicating allow us to get really cozy in our comfort zones, but real power comes from seeking to step out of them.

I suggest that each day you do something that widens that space for you. Call someone who seems intimidating, buy something that you need that costs more than you would ever have paid in the past, ask for something you want that you have been too frightened to ask for before. Take a risk a day—one small or bold stroke that will make you feel great once you've done it. Even if it doesn't work out the way you wanted it to, at least you've tried. You didn't sit back . . . powerless. Watch what starts to happen when you expand your comfort zone:

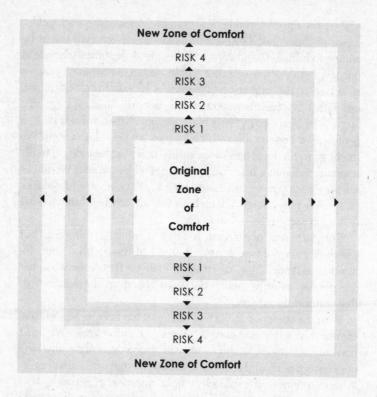

As the drawing shows, with each risk you take, with each time you move beyond what feels comfortable, you become more powerful. Your whole life expands to take in more of what there is in this world to experience. As your power builds, so does your confidence, so that stretching your comfort zone becomes easier and easier, despite any fear you may be experiencing. The magnitude of the risks you take also expands. In the beginning, for example, you may sign up for an online course after being out of school for 15 years. Ultimately you may enroll to get your graduate degree. You will be expanding . . . opening up . . . becoming bigger . . . but all at your own pace. As long as you are taking those risks—no matter how small—you are moving yourself to the right on the Pain-to-Power Chart.

Each night before you go to bed, plan the risk you are going to take the following day. Close your eyes, and in your mind's eye, practice doing it. This is called a visualization—the creation of a mental image of something in an effort to achieve what you want. Make your visualization as clear as you possibly can. Also, as you go through the day, be aware of where you find yourself hesitating, and start planning your future risks based on these observations. If you can push through the hesitation at the moment you recognize it, great. Remember that the more you expand your comfort zone, the more powerful you become.

PLEASE NOTE: The risks I am talking about do not include physically dangerous acts, such as speeding in a car or taking drugs. Nor do they include risks that infringe on the rights of other people, such as making an unwanted pass at someone or, for that matter, robbing a bank. Not only could you end up unpopular, dead, or in prison, but also you would be moving far to the left side of the Pain-to-Power Chart. These kinds of actions are not empowering because they do not have any integrity or love—for one's self or others—behind them. Without these ingredients, it is impossible to build your sense of self-worth. Hence your ability to handle fear would be greatly diminished.

So take only those risks each day that build your sense of self-worth. These are the risks that enhance your ability to deal with your fears. EXPAND! EXPAND! EXPAND!

Whether it feels like it or not, you already have more power than you could ever have imagined. We all have. When I speak of going from pain to power, I am not talking about pulling the power in from any outside source. Inside of you, just waiting to emerge, is an incredible source of energy that is more than sufficient for you to create a joyful and satisfying life. It isn't magic. It is only a process of tapping the energy already within you, though you may not be aware of it.

The exercises contained in this book are designed to lead you to this great source of power. Whether you do them or not is a good clue as to whether you are willing at this time to accept all that is within you. If you are not, don't berate yourself. Just make a commitment to keep working toward it. One way to do this is to read and reread this book and other personal-growth books until you rid yourself of the negative belief systems that are keeping you stuck in your powerlessness. Most of us are filled with old conditioning that is keeping us weak. It takes constant repetition for newer and healthier patterns to take hold.

You are innately designed to use your personal power. When you don't, you experience helplessness, paralysis, and depression—which is your clue that something is not working as it could.

You, like all of us, deserve everything that is wonderful and exciting in life. And those feelings emerge only when you get in touch with your powerful self.

you are in control you are in control

4.

Whether You Want It or Not . . . It's Yours

you are in control you are in control

Are you a "victim," or are you taking responsibility for your life? So many of us *think* we are taking responsibility for our own lives when we simply are not. The "victim" mentality is very subtle and takes many forms. Once you understand the concepts in this chapter you will better understand the dynamics of handling fear.

The idea of taking responsibility for your own life is probably not totally new to you. For years you have been bombarded with this message: TAKE RESPONSIBILITY FOR YOURSELF.

But I am convinced that most of us do not really understand what that means.

To most of us "independent" people, it has meant that we should get a job, earn enough money to support ourselves, and not depend on anyone else for our survival. That may or may not be part of it (I know many "dependent" people who understand the secret of taking responsibility for their experience of life), but it certainly doesn't hit the heart of the issue, which is much bigger, yet more invisible, than that. Let's look at a few examples.

Edward is an extremely wealthy, high-powered executive who lives in a constant state of anxiety. When I suggested that he get some professional help, he responded that if the people in his life would change, everything would be fine. If only his wife would be more loving, if only his boss wasn't always leaning on him, and if only his son would stop taking drugs—then he'd be fine. He feels there is no reason for him to get help; it's all *their* fault. Is he taking responsibility for his experience of life? Absolutely not!

Allen considers himself a reasonable person and open to new ideas, but when his son came out as transgender, you would have thought the world was ending. He was embarrassed and ashamed and he didn't want to talk about the subject to anyone, even his closest friends. It was eating him from the inside out. As if it were a personal affront, he kept asking himself, "How could his child do this to him?" Is he taking responsibility for his experience of life?

Mara is, by any measure, sitting on top of the world. She has a great job, lives in a lovely apartment, has many friends and love interests. Her continual complaint is about her ex-husband: he is making her life miserable, he has always been unfair to her, he never pays child support. Also, her son is turning against her and accusing her of being selfish . . . and on . . . and on . . . and on. Is she taking responsibility for her experience of life? Absolutely not!

I know many single or divorced people who are constantly complaining about their ex-partners, their bosses, their loneliness, how hard it is to meet anyone, and so on. I know many married people who are constantly lamenting about their children, their lack of money, their lack of communication with their partners, and so on. I know so many people who simply complain about everything nonstop.

Are any of these people really taking responsibility for their experience of life? Not at all! They are all, in some way, playing the role of victim. They have given their power to someone or something else. Keep in mind that when you give away your power, you move farther and farther to the left side of the Pain-to-Power Chart, and as a result you become paralyzed in your attempts to deal with fear.

On a more obvious level, if you're in a job you hate, if you're single and you want to be married, if you're in a lousy relationship and want to get out, if your children are causing you endless worry, and if, generally speaking, nothing seems to go the way you want it to go, you are also playing the role of victim. No wonder you feel fearful—victims are powerless!

THE TRUTH IS, YOU REALLY ARE IN CONTROL—IN TO-TAL CONTROL. For some reason, you are consciously or unconsciously choosing to be in that terrible job, you are choosing to hate the single life, you are choosing to stay in a destructive relationship, you are choosing to let your children drive you crazy, you are choosing to sabotage anything good in your life . . . or whatever else it may be for you. I know it is difficult to accept the fact that you are the cause of the feelings that take away your joy in life. It is very upsetting when you begin to see yourself as your own worst enemy. On the other hand, *this realization is your biggest blessing*. If you know you can create your own misery, it stands to reason that you can also create your own joy.

Since taking responsibility for your experience of life is an elusive concept, I will explain the components of a more powerful way of living. Note that I have been careful not to ask you to believe that you are responsible for all your experiences *in* life (although there are some who would argue that you are.) Rather, I ask you to believe you are the cause of all your experiences *of* life, meaning that you are the cause of your *reactions* to everything that happens to you. There is a lot more about this in the next chapter and in Chapter 9.

As you read the following seven definitions of taking responsibility, keep remembering that whenever you are not taking responsibility, you put yourself in a position of pain and hence decrease your ability to handle the fear in your life.

SEVEN DEFINITIONS OF TAKING RESPONSIBILITY

1. *Taking responsibility means never blaming anyone else for anything you are being, doing, having, or feeling.* "Never?" you say. "But this time it really is his fault" (or her fault, or the boss's fault, or my son's fault, or the economy's fault, or my mother's fault, or my father's fault, or my friend's fault!). "Really, it is!" If I missed anyone or anything, just add it to the list. Until you fully understand that *you*, and no one else, create what goes on in your head, you will never be in control of your life. Here are a few scenarios I've heard in my classes and workshops, and the questions these individuals had to ask themselves before they were able to move to a more powerful place.

Madeline

"Well, it certainly was my husband's fault that the past twenty-five years of my life have been so miserable!"

Why did you choose to stay? Why couldn't you take in any of the nice things he did for you instead of only finding fault? Why are you so filled with anger that he finds it impossible to communicate with you?

David

"Well, it certainly was my son's fault that I have gray hair, from worrying about him."

Why didn't you believe that he would find his own way? Why did you always need to rescue him? Why didn't you trust him? Why did you make him so much an extension of yourself that you expected too much from him? Why couldn't you just let him be who he is?

Tony

"Well, it certainly is the fault of the job market that I'm stuck in this crappy job."

Why can't you see that others are finding jobs even if the job market is so poor? Why are you not creating more satisfaction in the job you already have? Why aren't you even trying to find a new job? Why are you not asking for what you want in the job you are already in, instead of constantly complaining that nothing is right? Why aren't you committed to doing the best you can do?

Amina

"Well, it certainly is my family's fault that I'm not moving ahead in my career."

Why haven't you noticed that others with their own family responsibilities are going ahead with their dreams and their careers, and their families are doing just fine? Why haven't you carved out the time you know you need to expand your career? Why haven't you talked to your family about releasing you from some of your duties? Why haven't you taken up your spouse's offer to help you with the kids if you want to work? Why haven't you made any effort to gain some new skills that would really help you get a job you would love?

Lexi

"Well, it certainly is not my fault that I can't find anyone decent to date."

Why don't you try new ways to meet people? What are you looking for that makes it hard to meet the right person? Are you expecting perfection in someone else? Why are you waiting for the perfect mate to find you? Why are you giving up?

If you are feeling some pain from identifying with any of the stories above, good. It simply pinpoints an area on which you have to work. The point to remember is that when you blame any outside force for any of your experience of life, you are literally giving away all your power and thus creating pain, paralysis, and depression.

2. *Taking responsibility means not blaming yourself.* I know this sounds contradictory, but it is not. *Anything* that takes away your power or your pleasure makes you a victim. Don't make yourself a victim of yourself!

For some, this is more difficult than not blaming others. Once you become aware that you have created so much of your own unhappiness, you may have a tendency to punish yourself and put yourself down: "There I am, messing up my life again. I'm hopeless. When will I ever learn?"

This, again, is not taking responsibility for your experience of life. It is important to understand that you have always done the best you possibly could, given the person you were at any particular moment in time. Now that you are learning a new way of thinking, you can begin to perceive things differently and possibly change many of your actions. There is absolutely no need to be upset with your past, present, or future behavior. It is all simply part of the learning process—the process of moving yourself from pain to power. And it takes time. You must be patient with yourself. There is never any need to be down on yourself. Nothing is your "fault." Yes, you cause your own unhappiness, but this is no reason to cast blame. You're simply on the path toward greater self-fulfillment, and it is a lengthy process of trial and error.

This is a great opportunity to think about your Pain-to-Power Vocabulary. When you tell yourself you're "hopeless," it will be easier to blame yourself than if you tell yourself that "this is a learning experience." Remember that words have power, and how you speak to yourself reflects whether or not you are taking responsibility for your experiences.

3. *Taking responsibility means being aware of where and when you are* not *taking responsibility so that you can eventually change.* When you have strong negative emotions, such as annoyance, anger, anxiety, hatred, envy, depression, and so many others, allow them to trigger new awareness. You can create negative emotional states and give yourself a lot of reasons to be miserable and complain when you are letting yourself be a victim.

It took years before I realized that the place I played the victim role most often was with the men in my life. I remember many evenings of complaining, for countless hours, with my girlfriends about the grief the men in my life were causing me.

Those "jerks," as I so self-righteously called them, were always doing something to take away my happiness. One was always late, one was incredibly stingy, one didn't make enough money, one loved to play golf too much, one wouldn't get a divorce, and so on. I was able to build up incredible anger and resentment about them. Hours and hours on the phone of, "Would you believe he actually . . ." Naturally, my loyal friends shared my drama as I shared their upsets about their relationships. It was a Moan and Groan Society. We never seemed to tire of each other's stories. No wonder: we fed each other the martyrdom we were obviously enjoying, and we always got to be right! The payoff was that we didn't have to create our own happiness—we could simply blame others for not giving it to us.

During this time, I was certain I was taking responsibility for my life. Just like my friend Mara, I was making a wonderful living. I had a great apartment. I was totally "independent." But I *wasn't* taking responsibility for my life. I was still expecting someone else in my life to "make me happy." I finally learned there is only one person in the world who can make me happy, and that is ME! Ironically, only through this realization was I able, for the first time, to have a wonderfully nurturing relationship.

Now I know that when I am angry at my husband, I simply have to ask myself, "What am I not doing in my life that I could be doing that I am blaming him for not doing for me?" (Read that one again!) I am now quickly able to tune in to what it is. Either I'm being obsessive about money, or I'm feeling insecure, or I'm not creating enough activity for myself, or I'm expecting him to make "all better" something I'm not handling well, or whatever.

Once I realize what I am doing, I can get into the task of correcting it. As I correct what needs to be handled in my life, all my anger toward others disappears. My daughter, Leslie, recently commented on how fantastic my marriage is. "Yes," I said, "it's amazing how perfect Mark becomes when I stop expecting him to handle my life!"

This is not to say that you aren't entitled to have your basic needs met by your partner—the need to be supported in your growth, the need to be nurtured at times, the need to know there is caring on your spouse's part—but when you are not handling your life, no amount of caring and nurturing is enough. You become a bottomless pit. The partner in your life could stand on their head for you, as some of the men in my life tried to do, but it is never enough.

I might add that if someone is not supplying your basic needs to be nurtured and loved, certainly you would serve yourself by leaving. But first you must ask yourself, "Is it that my partner is so terrible, or is it simply that I am not taking responsibility for my experience of life?" If you are satisfied that you simply do not choose to spend your life with this person, then it is also taking responsibility to move on with the intention of finding a more compatible partner.

If you do choose to move on, one clue that you are truly taking responsibility is when you feel little or no anger toward this person. You realize that you chose to be there in the past and you are now choosing to leave. Nothing is the other's fault. They are doing the best they can, given their level of personal growth. Anger is your clue that you are not taking responsibility.

A relationship with another is only one area where you can give away your power. It is important to look at all other areas of your life as well, to determine where you are not taking responsibility. Your clue will be any one of the following signs:

Anger	Impatience
Upset	Joylessness
Blaming others	Fatigue
Pain	Attempt to control others
Lack of focus	Obsessiveness
Self-pity	Addictions
Envy	Judgmental attitude
Helplessness	Disappointment
Constant state of limbo	Jealousy

This is not a complete list, but you get the idea. Whenever you feel any of these, determine what *you* are not doing in your life that is causing the telltale sign. You will be surprised how easy it is to locate where you are abdicating responsibility.

4. *Taking responsibility means handling the Chatterbox.* This is the little voice inside, the voice that tries to drive you crazy—and often succeeds! I'll bet some of you don't even know it's there (I was shocked when I became aware of it), but I promise you it holds the key to all your fears. It's the voice that heralds doom, lack, and losing. We're so used to its presence, we often don't even notice it is talking to us. If you are not aware of your Chatterbox, it sounds something like this:

I am so tired of being alone. It's really depressing when all my friends have dates or spouses or partners and they are always going out someplace interesting. If I join them, I'm the third wheel or even the fifth wheel. No one wants to be with a third or fifth wheel all the time. I feel so conspicuous. I'm sure everyone notices that I'm on my own . . . again. I'm a walking disaster. No wonder no one wants to go out with me. I wouldn't want to go out with me. What do I possibly have to offer? I'm such a loser. I don't even know how my friends can stand me. I certainly can't stand me. Maybe if I dressed better or got a new haircut. Maybe I need a cooler look to create a good impression. Maybe that would help. But then they would talk to me and know for sure that I'm a loser. Maybe that's why I always picked losers too. Like that date I had last month, the guy was so gross, he picked his teeth at dinner, yet he had the nerve to say that he wasn't that into me. Seriously. He's the one with hygiene issues. Meeting someone you click with is so hard. I wonder what's wrong with me. I just am so tired of going home disappointed; I'd rather not even bother to try to meet someone anymore. But if I stop trying, then I'll really never meet anyone. Maybe that's what I deserve. To be alone . . . .

Or this:

I'm really angry at my boss for not including me in the meeting this morning. He really doesn't appreciate all the work I do for him. The others spend their day loafing

*and they get invited to the meeting. Maybe I'll try loafing
and see if he likes that better. It really doesn't pay to give
your all to a job. You never get rewarded for all the hard
work. It just pays to be a big manipulator, like all the rest.
An honest hard worker is just not appreciated anymore.
I'll show him. I'll look around for another job. But the
job market is so lousy right now, I'd never find anything.
I wish I had completed my master's degree—then I'd
have a better chance. I'm really stuck here . . . no one is
hiring people over 40 anymore. It's all in who you know.
If my parents had had money, I would have been able to
socialize with people who have some clout. I really feel
used. I can't believe they excluded me from the meeting.
Who does he think he is? This kind of thing always
happens to me . . .*

No wonder so many of us hate being alone and can't stop texting or can't be in a room without turning on the television or
constantly playing music for company. Anything to escape such
insanity! Be assured that this "insanity" seems to be an unavoid-
able phase in the growth process. We are all victims of our Chatterbox at some point in our lives.

Now that you know it exists, you will also notice that you can't
seem to turn it off—at least not yet. The good news is that there
are very effective ways to get rid of this kind of negativity, which
will be discussed in later chapters. For now, simply notice that
your Chatterbox is making you a victim, and commit yourself to
replacing it with a loving voice. You don't have to hang out with
enemies, even if they are within you. By the way, once you get rid
of the negativity your Chatterbox brings, you will really begin to
enjoy being alone.

5. *Taking responsibility means being aware of payoffs that
keep you "stuck."* Payoffs explain why we choose to perpetuate
what we don't want in our lives. Once you understand payoffs,
your behavior will make much more sense to you. Let me give
you a few examples.

Jeanne

Jeanne was feeling horribly stuck in her job and wanted desperately to get out. She viewed herself as a victim. Poor Jeanne! Her Chatterbox constantly played the "if only" game. If only the job market were a little better, she wouldn't have a problem. If only she had better skills, there would be more opportunity. What was really keeping Jean at her job? What were the payoffs?

By remaining a victim, Jeanne had clearly become comfortable. She didn't have to face possible rejection in her search for a new job. Although she hated her job, it was easy. She knew she could handle it; she didn't have to question her competence. She put in her hours and didn't have to expend any additional energy. And the job was relatively secure.

Once Jeanne became aware of all her payoffs, she had at least three choices. The first was to stay where she was and continue to be miserable. The second was to stay where she was and choose to enjoy her job. The third was to choose to find a more satisfying job.

What did she ultimately do? After recognizing the payoffs for what they were, she was able to break away and find a new job. As long as she was in the victim mode, she was stuck. As soon as she realized she was choosing to stay because of the payoffs, *and not because of her "if onlys,"* she was able to make positive changes in her life.

Kevin

Kevin had been separated from his wife for five years. Although he had found someone else he wanted to marry, he was not able to tell his wife and children that he wanted a divorce. When the new woman threatened to leave, he sought professional help. The "victim" story his Chatterbox was telling him was that his wife would kill herself, his children would never talk to him again, and his parents would disown him. Poor Kevin! He really believed all this on a conscious level and was paralyzed with guilt.

With the help of a therapist, it did not take him long to see that the real problem was his own fear of letting go. Though he no longer loved his wife, she unconsciously represented a psychological "place to come home to," and he was frightened to sever the tie permanently. That was his payoff for staying stuck.

As soon as Kevin was able to see that his own irrational fear was stopping him, he immediately started proceedings to divorce his wife. Naturally, his wife did not kill herself, his children never stopped talking to him, and his parents didn't disown him. They wondered what had taken him so long! The point is that once he recognized that his payoffs were the reason he was choosing to remain in the marriage, his guilt disappeared and he was able to take action.

Tanya

Tanya was always sick, which interfered greatly with many of the things she wanted to do in life. She truly saw herself as a "poor thing" endowed with an unhealthy body. A full-fledged victim if you ever saw one! In one of my workshops, I asked the group to list the payoffs for staying "stuck" in whatever it was that was bothering them. Tanya could find no payoffs for being sick all the time . . . until the group helped her out.

They pointed out to her that her illness got her a lot of attention and that it kept her from having to put herself out there in the world and take any risks. She denied it at first, but finally was able to acknowledge that there was some truth in what they were saying.

Tanya had never looked at her unhealthiness as manipulation, though her unconscious knew exactly what it was doing. As a child, illness was the only device that got her any attention. Tanya's awareness of the payoffs was the impetus she needed to turn her life around. Realizing that she was possibly creating her attitude toward her ill health, she made a lot of changes in her life.

First, she completely changed her diet and started a fitness program. Just as important—perhaps more so—she asked the significant others in her life to help her by "rewarding" her only when she was well and ignoring her when she was sick. They obliged after a little practice. She began creating work goals for herself and pushing herself to meet them, even when she was unwell. She began doing many of the positive exercises in this book—such as using affirmations and inspirational audios and podcasts. She began going to workshops and joining online classes to better understand the issues of responsibility and personal choice.

When she fully realized her payoffs for being ill, Tanya was able to choose: Did she want to get attention for being sick all her life, or did she want to find a more satisfying way of relating to people and to her life goals? Did she always want to be an observer of life rather than a participant? She chose the latter . . . and sickness is no longer as big an issue in her life.

From these case studies, you can see the power that hidden payoffs can have in our lives. They are not difficult to discover once you realize they exist. It's simply a matter of sitting down with a pencil and paper and listing them. Sometimes they are obvious to others, but masked from your own vision. If you can't find them, ask a friend to help. You might be surprised to discover that your friends know more about your motives than you do.

6. Taking responsibility means figuring out what you want in life and acting on it. Set your goals—then go out and work toward them. Take charge of your life.

Figure out what kind of space you would like to live in . . . then create it. It doesn't take a lot of money to create a peaceful, loving home for yourself.

Look around and see who you would love to include in your circle of friends . . . then contact them and make plans to get together. Don't sit around waiting for them to get in touch with you.

Consider your body. Determine what you need to do to feel

healthy . . . then make it happen. Change your eating habits—vegan, paleo, vegetarian, gluten-free—we have plenty of options these days. The same for exercise—yoga, boxing, spinning, salsa, stand-up paddleboarding. Whatever makes you move.

Most of us do not "sculpt" our lives. We accept what comes our way . . . then we gripe about it. Many of us spend our lives waiting—waiting for the perfect partner, waiting for the perfect job, waiting for perfect friends to come along. There is no need to wait for anyone to give you anything in your life. You have the power to create what you need. Given commitment, clear goals, and action, it's just a matter of time.

7. *Taking responsibility means being aware of the multitude of choices you have in any given situation.* One of my students put it this way: "From the time my alarm clock rings, I have an hour and a half alone and I realize it's all up to me what the day is going to start like. It's up to me whether I'm going to open the shades and let the light in or mess around in the dark. It's my choice to lie in bed and say, 'Yuck, I don't want to get up and go to work. I didn't finish the report I'm supposed to have ready today.' Or it's my choice to lie in bed and give myself positive self-talk and look forward to the coming day. It's my choice to put the music on and dance around the apartment instead of putting on the negativity of the news or listening to my negative Chatterbox. It's up to me whether I'm going to worry about how my body is not in shape or whether I'm going to tell myself I am in the process of creating a great body. The whole day is up to me!"

As you go through each day, it is important to realize that at every moment you are choosing the way you feel. When a difficult situation comes into your life, it is possible to tune in to your mind and say, "Okay, choose." Are you going to make yourself miserable or content? Are you going to visualize scarcity or abundance? Are you going to put yourself down for getting angry with your partner, or are you simply going to notice what insecurity you were feeling at the time and discuss it with them? The choice is definitely yours. Pick the one that contributes the most to your positivity and growth.

Here are some other kinds of choices:

> *Your friend decides not to go with you on the trip you had planned together. You're really angry . . . OR . . . You understand she has her reasons, and you find someone else to share the trip, or you go alone and have a blast!*
>
> *Your spouse is an alcoholic. You spend your whole life trying to change them or scold them . . . OR . . . You attend Al-Anon meetings and learn to change yourself.*
>
> *A bout of flu has caused you to miss the big meeting you were scheduled to attend. You are sure this means the end of your whole career . . . OR . . . You realize you have limitless ways of creating a successful career for yourself.*
>
> *Your visit to sunny California is filled with torrents of rain. You lament your bad luck for the entire trip . . . OR . . . You find ways to make it a great vacation anyway.*
>
> *You finally meet an online date for the first time in person and you find that's she's not right for you. You decide to give up dating altogether . . . OR . . . You chalk it up to experience and try again to meet someone new.*
>
> *Your holiday with your family is a chore since you and they have polar opposite opinions on politics. You stand your ground, making everyone uncomfortable around the dinner table . . . OR . . . You try to see their point of view and ask them to listen to yours.*

By now you can really see that the choice is yours. As you continue to read, you will further your ability to place yourself on the upside of any given situation. Keep in mind that this way of thinking doesn't excuse inappropriate or abusive behavior on the part of others in your life. It simply allows you to have a more satisfying life. Fully taking responsibility for your experience of life is a long process that requires much practice. I'm still working on it daily after many years . . . and each day my life gets better and better and better. The point is simply to begin. You will start to feel better immediately.

SIX TOOLS TO HELP YOU
FIND YOUR POWER

The following six tools will help you feel noticeably more powerful in the face of your fears:

1. List the Payoffs

List all the payoffs you get from staying stuck in some aspect of your life. What don't you have to face? What don't you have to do? What comfort do you get? What image do you get to hold on to? Be as honest with yourself as you possibly can. When you are aware of what you are doing, you will automatically discard a lot of your robotlike behavior. You will lead yourself instead of being led.

2. Know Your Options

Be aware of all the options you have during the course of a given day. When you are confronted with a difficult situation, sit down and write in a notebook all the possible ways you can act and feel about it. Close your eyes and picture yourself happy about it . . . then sad about it . . . then annoyed . . . then seeing what's humorous in it . . . then heavy . . . then light . . . and so on. You will begin to see how easy it is to change your point of view—hence, your feelings. You are in control.

Each time you are upset, be conscious of the alternatives available to you. Again, make it a game. In no way should you put yourself down for being upset. It's a great clue as to where you need to begin taking responsibility.

3. Listen to Yourself

Start noticing what you say in conversations with friends. See if it includes a lot of complaining about other people, or just a lot of complaining in general. If you notice this to be the case, ask yourself why you are really upset. Do you really have a reason to complain?

For example, you might grumble, "Would you believe that Jill was late for dinner again? We had the biggest fight—right in the restaurant." If this sounds familiar, see if you can turn the situation around so that you learn something new about yourself. For example, "I notice that when Jill is late, I begin to feel really angry. I wonder why I feel that way? I think it's because she doesn't seem to have any respect for my time. On the other hand, part of me likes it. It makes me feel superior always to have something to gripe about . . ."

4. Choose Your Experiences

In a notebook, list the many choices available to you that can change presently upsetting experiences into positive ones. Using the example of Jill's lateness, what choices could you make?

You could stop meeting with her; arrive later, knowing she will be late; bring some interesting reading material; relax. If meeting on time is essential, you could simply tell her that if she is not there by an agreed-upon hour, you will not wait. When you are in control of your actions and reactions, there is no reason for anger.

The key is not to blame others for your being upset. This is not to condone the behavior of others, but simply not to allow it to be the source of your upset.

In every situation there are dozens of ways to change your point of view. You could make yourself an impartial outside observer, or you could pretend that you are the other person who is causing the problem. You get the picture. Make this another game—the "change your point of view" strategy. Share it with someone you trust; having a "growth buddy" can be very nourishing and illuminating.

5. Find the Gift in Everything

Begin to look at the gifts you have received from what you have always considered a "bad" situation. For example, if you are still hurting from your divorce, begin to focus on the good things you had during the marriage and the good things that have come about as a result of the divorce, such as new friends, new ways of dealing with money, freedom, less dependency. If you were passed over for a promotion, focus on the fact that the next time you apply, you will have that much more experience to offer, or that the loss solidified the feeling that it's time to look for a new job. Recognize the gift in any negative experience and acknowledge it.

6. Ditch the Criticism

This one is really tough! See if you can go one week without criticizing anyone or complaining about anything. You will be surprised how difficult this is. You will also be surprised to learn how much complaining and criticizing you do.

By the way, when you ultimately stop putting down other people in your life, it may seem as if you have nothing left to talk about with your friends. Griping is a habit and needs to be replaced by something more positive. This takes a bit of time and ingenuity, but it will be far more satisfying and joyful.

SEVEN WAYS TO RECLAIM YOUR POWER

1. Avoid casting blame on an external force for your negative feelings about your life. Nothing outside yourself can control your thinking or your actions.

2. Avoid blaming yourself for not being in control. You are doing the best you can, and you are on the way to reclaiming your power.

3. Be aware of when and where you are playing the victim role. Learn the clues that tell you that you are not being responsible for what you are being, having, doing, or feeling.

4. Familiarize yourself with your biggest enemy—your Chatterbox. Use the exercises and tools throughout the book to replace your Chatterbox with a loving, positive internal friend.

5. Figure out the payoffs that keep you "stuck." Paradoxically, once you find them, you will probably be able to quickly become "unstuck."

6. Determine what you want in life and act on it. Stop waiting for someone to give it to you. You'll be waiting a long time.

7. Be aware of the many choices you have—in both actions and feelings—in any situation that comes your way. Choose the path that contributes to your growth and makes you feel at peace with yourself and others.

5.

The Return of
the Optimist

I am a strong and worthy person I am a strong and worthy person

"**H**ow can you be so optimistic?" How many times has someone tried to put you down with these words when you were trying to look at the brighter side of things? For many years I never questioned that being an optimist was a bad thing. That idea was unconsciously hammered into my head.

Having dinner with a friend one evening, I fervently tried to make her see the positive side of something she fervently viewed as negative. Suddenly she disdainfully remarked, "You're beginning to sound like Pollyanna." (Pollyanna was the heroine of a book and movie who was known for making the best out of everything that happened to her.) Much to my friend's surprise and mine, I blurted out, "What's so terrible about Pollyanna, anyway? What's wrong with feeling good about life despite the obstacles in your way? What's wrong with looking at the sunshine instead of seeing gloom and doom? What's wrong with trying to see good in everything? *Nothing* is wrong with it!" I asserted. "In fact," I added incredulously, "why would anyone *resist* thinking that way?"

And resist we do! Positive thinking is one of the most difficult of all concepts to get across to people. When I present my ideas on positive thinking in my workshops and classes, many of my students respond immediately with, "Oh, that's not realistic!" Yet when I question them about what makes negative thinking more realistic, they cannot give me an answer. There is an automatic assumption that negative is realistic and positive is unrealistic. Upon inspection, this is pure nonsense.

Seneca, the Roman philosopher and statesman, wrote a very long time ago, "We suffer more often in imagination than in reality." Things haven't changed much over the past 2,000 years, have they? It is reported that over 90% of what we worry about never happens. That means that our negative worries have less than a 10% chance of being correct. If this is so, isn't being positive more realistic than being negative? Think about your own life. I'll wager that most of what you worry about never happens. So are you being realistic when you worry all the time? No!

If you think about it, the important issue is not which is more realistic, but rather, *"Why be miserable when you can be happy?"* If being an optimist creates a happier world for you and those around you, why hesitate for one more moment?

Let's look at examples of these two attitudes. When Jennifer and Marcy were in their mid-40s, each lost her partner suddenly. Jennifer immediately took on the mantle of tragedy. For years, she solicited sympathy from everyone, until it reached the point where no one wanted to be in her company. She then had "proof" that single women never get invited anywhere. She convinced herself that she would never find anyone to love her again, and naturally, that's the reality her attitude and behavior were creating for her. After her husband's death, she had only a small amount of savings, not enough to really live on. So she decided to supplement her savings with a job. She managed to find an average part-time position in retail, but she was convinced that no one would hire her for a better, full-time job because of her age. She went to a few interviews, but with her lack of enthusiasm and skepticism, she understandably never got a better job. Her negativity created a "realistic" life of misery.

Marcy, on the other hand, took an optimistic approach after her partner's death. Following a period of mourning, she picked herself up and started all over again. She was one of those individuals who truly believes that one can create good from anything. She too was left without any extra money, and she determined that it was now time to go out and earn her own keep.

Although Marcy hadn't had a full-time job since her children were born, she was confident that a place for her existed in the job market. She had always done volunteer fundraising and liked it immensely. On the basis of her experience as a volunteer, she applied to be an assistant in the fundraising department of a medium-sized charity. Within two years, she found herself totally in charge. Throughout this period she was feeling a sense of expansion and growth she had never felt before. Although she still misses her partner immeasurably, she realizes she has grown enormously as a result of having to create a new life and make it on her own.

Unlike Jennifer's friends, Marcy's never excluded her from any of their plans. Why would they? She always brought an incredible sense of enthusiasm and exuberance to life. The way she turned her tragedy into triumph served as an inspiration to everyone. Her positive outlook created a very "realistic" life of joy and satisfaction.

Nothing is realistic or unrealistic—there is only what we think about any given situation. *We create our own reality*.

What does this have to do with fear? Everything! Remember, to handle fear is to move from a position of pain to one of power. Although both women had their fears, Jennifer held hers from a position of pain, whereas Marcy held hers from a position of power. Jennifer's fears resulted in stagnation; Marcy's fears resulted in growth.

Jennifer still worries about not having enough friends, about dying alone, about running out of money. Her heaviness is ominous. She truly lives her life on the left side of the Pain-to-Power Chart—helpless, depressed, and paralyzed.

Marcy's fears, on the other hand, led to her raising more than enough money for her organization, doing a good job on a podcast, launching a public outreach plan, and other successes. Her fears have a totally different quality than Jennifer's. She lives on the right side of the Pain-to-Power Chart—at ease in her world, excited, and motivated. There is absolutely no question that learning to think more positively will pull you closer and closer to finding your own power.

I learned an amazing way to demonstrate the effectiveness of positive versus negative thinking, which I have often used in my workshops. I ask someone to come up and stand facing the rest of the class. Today it's a young woman. After making sure she has no problems with her arms, I ask my volunteer to make a fist and extend one arm out to the side. I then tell her to resist, with as much strength as she can muster, as I stand facing her and attempt to push her arm down with my outstretched hand. Not once have I succeeded in pushing a student's arm down on my initial trial.

I then ask her to put her arm down, close her eyes, and repeat ten times the negative statement "I am a weak and unworthy person." I tell her really to get into the feel of that statement. When she has repeated it ten times, I ask her to open her eyes and extend her arm again exactly as she had before. I remind her to resist as hard as she can. Immediately, I am able to bring down her arm. It is as though all strength has left her.

I wish I had recorded the expressions on my volunteers' faces when they find it impossible to resist my pressure. A few have made me do it again. "I wasn't ready!" is their plea. Lo and behold, the same thing happens on the second try—the arm goes right down with little resistance. They are dumbfounded.

I then ask the volunteer once again to close her eyes, and repeat ten times the positive statement "I am a strong and worthy person." Again I tell her to really get into the feeling of the words. Then I ask her to extend her arm and resist my pressure. To her amazement (and everyone else's) I cannot budge the arm. In fact, it is more steadfast than the first time I tried to push it down.

If I continue interspersing positive with negative, the same results occur. I can push the arm down after the negative statement, but I am not able to push it down after the positive statement. By the way—for you skeptics out there—I tried this experiment when I was unaware of what the volunteer was saying. I left the room, and the class decided whether the statement should be negative or positive. It didn't matter. Weak words meant a weak arm. Strong words meant a strong arm.

This is a stunning demonstration of the power of the words we speak. Positive words make us physically strong; negative words make us physically weak. The amazing aspect of this experiment is that it doesn't matter if we *believe* the words or not. The mere uttering of them makes our inner self believe them. It is as though the inner self doesn't know what is true and what is false. It doesn't judge. It only reacts to what it is fed. When the words "I am weak" come in, our inner self instructs the rest of us, "He wants to be weak today." When the words "I am strong" come in, the instruction to your body is "He wants to be strong today."

What does all this tell you? STOP FEEDING YOURSELF NEG-ATIVE THOUGHTS. Negative thoughts take away your power . . . and thus make you more paralyzed due to your fear.

As you know, positive thinking is not a new concept. Aside from Pollyanna, Norman Vincent Peale, Napoleon Hill, Maxwell Maltz, and others popularized the concept many years ago. Their books are still available today. Every year many more books about positive thinking are published. So, why don't people think more *positively*? Why do they *resist* it? My guess is that people don't understand what being a positive thinker requires. It takes a special commitment and requires a great deal of practice. And once you get it all down thoroughly, a maintenance program is a must. I know of no one who has been able to make "positive" a permanent way of thinking without practice. Such people may exist; I simply haven't met them. In my experience, if you don't practice, you lose the skill. This is the point most people don't seem to understand.

I know it doesn't seem fair that you automatically become negative when you stop practicing the positive. I liken it to exercise. Once you get your body in shape, you can't stop working out. Within a short time your muscles start losing tone, and where you once could do 50 sit-ups, 20 is now your maximum. You must keep at it.

The intellect acts in the same way. When problem solving, stimulating discussion, or reading is a part of your daily life, your mind stays sharp. After a two-week vacation of lounging on the beach, your brain feels soggy. It takes quite a few days to get your brain back in shape. Clearly, certain aspects of ourselves need constant reinforcement, and a positive mental attitude is just one of them.

I know most people resist the fact that constant practice is required, but we aren't positive thinkers by nature. It might help to remember that your shower, your makeup, and your shave also don't last, yet you don't have any resistance to starting your day with showering, putting on your makeup, or shaving. These are refreshing activities—and so is positive thinking. In fact, it feels wonderful!

So here you are, a blob of negativity. How do you even begin to turn around those miserable thoughts that take away your power? You begin by doing the same thing you would do if your body were out of shape. You create an exercise program—in this case, to retrain your mind. To do so, *you must take action.*

Before giving you a suggested action plan, I recommend that you have on hand the following items to make your daily routine more efficient and certainly more pleasurable:

1. An audio player, your phone, a tablet, or whatever technology suits you best for "portable" listening.

2. An array of audio material for creating a positive view of life. We are so fortunate in today's world to have so many accessible formats! There are audios, videos and podcasts on affirmations, relaxation, meditation, motivation, and visualization, as well as inspirational apps that will be wonderful for helping you along your journey. Also, many uplifting books are now available in an e-book or other audio format. Once you realize the benefits you'll receive from such listening material, you will take joy in building an extensive library.

3. Positive books that inspire and motivate. I suggest that you buy your books instead of borrowing them from the library or reading them on an e-reader. The reason for this is that you will want to underline and write in the books and reread them over and over again. You will want to "own" these books in every sense of the word. They provide an incredible support system that is there for you at all times. I can't think of a better investment to help you create a better life. I have a LARGE collection of books that I have read and reread many times over, while highlighting certain passages and writing my notes and thoughts in the margins. And as I learn and grow, I can look back and see what struck me as important in the past, what is important to me now, and how far I have come with the passage of time. The important thing is: BEGIN YOUR PERSONAL LIBRARY OF INSPIRATION NOW!

4. Index cards or sticky notes, or a mobile phone app that will send you reminders to open yourself up to the universe and think positive thoughts during the day.

5. Positive quotes. Find those that really touch you in some way. Some very effective quotes for me are:

> *"Ships in harbor are safe, but that's not what ships are built for."*
>
> —John Shedd

> *"The best way out is always through."*
>
> —Helen Keller

> *"I'm not a failure if I don't make it . . . I'm a success because I tried."*
>
> —Unknown

> *"Considering how dangerous everything is, nothing is really very frightening!"*
>
> —Gertrude Stein

> *"Feel the fear . . . and do it anyway!"*
>
> —Susan Jeffers

You can also follow me on Twitter at @SusanJeffers and Instagram to get daily inspirational quotes and affirmations!

Write each quote on an individual index card or note. Then put them all over the place—on your mirrors, your desk, the refrigerator door, in your car, on your schedule, and so on. Change the screen saver on your computer to show your favorite quotes as a slideshow. Or you can put your quotes on the home screen of your mobile phone.

If you are artistic, make decorative art with your quotes to hang on your wall. Or buy one of those wonderful posters with inspirational sayings and use it to decorate.

You may want to put one quote that really "speaks" to you in many places, so that wherever you turn, it's there as a reminder.

You will find that your quotes will change often as you move ahead with your life. Different ideas are meaningful at different times. Just keep changing the quotes. Be creative; try to bring some lightness to the task. As the humorist Jan Marshall said,

"Not a shred of evidence exists that life is serious!" Go overboard and be outrageous until friends ask you what's going on. Really have fun with this.

6. Affirmations. What is an affirmation? An affirmation is self-talk in its highest form. Remember the power of self-talk in the arm experiment? An affirmation is one of your greatest tools and the easiest and cheapest to use.

An affirmation is *a positive statement that something is already happening*. It's not happening in the future, but right now. Here are a few:

> *I am breaking through old patterns and moving forward*
> *with my life.*
> *I relax, knowing I can handle it all.*
> *I stand tall and take responsibility for my life.*
> *I know that I count and I act as if I do.*
> *I spread warmth and love everywhere I go.*
> *I let go and I trust it's all happening perfectly.*
> *I peacefully allow my life to unfold.*
> *I am finding the gift in all experiences.*
> *I am powerful and I am loving and I have nothing to fear.*
> *I focus on my many blessings.*

These are just a few to get you started. I am such a strong believer in affirmations that I have created three affirmation audios: *Inner Talk for a Confident Day, Inner Talk for Peace of Mind*, and *Inner Talk for a Love That Works* (available via SusanJeffers .com). Listening to these audios will certainly build up your repertoire of affirmations . . . as you build up your sense of confidence, peace, and love.

There are some things to remember about affirmations:

Always state affirmations in the present.

> **Wrong:** I will handle my fears.
> **Right:** I am now handling my fears.

*Always phrase affirmations in the positive, rather than
the negative.*

Wrong: I am no longer putting myself down.
Right: I am becoming more confident every day.

Select affirmations that feel right to you at a given time. What
feels right changes as your situation and mood change.

Now what do you do with all of these tools? I will illustrate by going through a typical day, putting these positive thinking tools to
use. The whole point of the program can be summed up in three
words: OUTTALK YOUR NEGATIVITY. And, as you probably already know, this is a challenge.

That internal Chatterbox has incredible staying power. It will
resist in every way it can in order to maintain its power over you.
Once you have that little voice under control, you've got it made.
At that point, positive thinking will become more automatic, so
that just a few daily reminders will suffice to keep you uplifted.
But in the beginning it's got to be full speed ahead! So let's go
through your first day of outtalking your Chatterbox.

BEGINNER'S INTENSIVE FOR POSITIVE THINKING

1. As you begin to awaken, begin your affirmation on the
device of your choice. Remember to choose it the night before
and have it teed up for your morning. An affirmation offers you
a wonderful way to start the day (*Inner Talk for a Confident Day*
would work beautifully here). Or you can choose a meditation, a
motivational or inspirational talk, or an audiobook or podcast as
an alternative. What great times we live in for learning and growing! As you begin listening, lie there with your eyes closed and let
the powerful and loving thoughts sink in. You have to admit this
certainly beats lying there thinking about how you don't want to
get up and face all the lousy and annoying things you have to do
all day.

2. As you get out of bed, pay attention to the positive quotes you've surrounded yourself with—on the wall, the refrigerator, your mirror, and so on. You might want to chuckle a bit at what it takes for the human race to make itself feel good!

3. As you dress, it's a great time to play some music that makes your heart sing. It could be relaxation music like a wind chime with ocean waves in the background, or rock music with a hard thumping beat, or a classical string quartet . . . whatever feels right for you at a given moment.

Also, as you get ready, begin to repeat the affirmations you have chosen for the day. A great place to repeat your affirmations is in front of the mirror. Repeat them for a few moments and continue throughout the day whenever negativity tries to enter your thinking. It requires vigilance to notice the negativity is there. It sneaks in so quietly. But as soon as you are aware of it, begin replacing this negativity with your affirmations. Don't let the little voice take over. *Outtalk your Chatterbox!* I promise you that with practice the negative voice will be the rarity and the positive voice the norm. Just believe that constant repetition will do the trick eventually.

Note: In the beginning, I suggest that you do not turn on the television or computer and listen to the news first thing in the day, if that is your habit. The presentation of the news is overwhelmingly negative. For the time being, let your chosen positive voice be the only news you hear as you prepare for the happenings of the day. If it is your habit to read the newspaper or read the news on a device as you eat breakfast, read one of your inspirational self-help books or stream a motivational video instead.

While teaching a fear class in New York, as an experiment I instructed my students to stay away from the news entirely for a certain period of time. They were surprised at the positive difference it made in their lives. Instead of talking with friends about how miserable the world situation was, they began sharing the positive ideas they developed, and their conversations became more uplifting and exciting.

Once you've acquired the positive thinking habit, you can resume reading and listening to the news. You may find you have developed a more constructive approach to the media, seeing in "bad news" opportunities to begin taking responsibility for yourself and your community.

4. If you exercise daily, this is an opportune time to pump in your positive thinking. Affirmations such as "I can feel the energy coursing through my body" and "I am creating a beautiful, healthy day" will make your exercise routine far more effective.

5. Breakfast is over and it is now time to get yourself to work. I live in Los Angeles and I often hear people lamenting about the time they have to spend in their cars. Not me! I have made my car my "temple of learning" and I can't wait to get into it. As soon as I turn on the motor, I turn on one of my audiobooks. I listen to either motivational or inspirational messages. Or I listen to stirring music. This is time that some people see as wasted but I see as immensely productive. Without my drive, I lose out on a lot of listening time.

Note: Do not use relaxation or meditation materials, or open social media apps in the car, for obvious reasons. With today's traffic congestion and people texting and not paying attention, you need to stay alert.

If you take public transportation, use a car service, or walk to work, you have it even better. You can listen to any type of inspirational or meditation audio and bliss out as much as you want (as long as you don't miss your stop or get distracted in a crosswalk). Or, if you prefer not to listen to anything, then simply repeat your affirmations over and over again, no matter how you travel.

If you are home during the day or if you work from home, you are in luck, because you can play your positive messages all day as you do your work or household tasks. If you have small children at home, think about the positive impact these affirmations will have on their young and impressionable minds.

6. As you walk into your work space, be aware of the positive messages you have already placed there. Again, chuckle to yourself. It helps you to lighten up about *everything*!

7. Pick one special affirmation for the day. Then write it in your schedule, or diary, or note it on your phone or computer. If you are running short of affirmations, choose one that feels right for you from my "Inner Talk" books or audios. Or, you can visit my website or my Twitter page and use the affirmations that are posted daily. Every time you refer to your schedule or notes, say the affirmation at least ten times. You can also place a special affirmation on your desk where it is constantly visible. Right now the affirmation on my desk is "It's all happening perfectly." It is there to remind me that no matter what happens relative to any situation in my life, I will learn and grow from it all. A great reminder, indeed!

8. Unless you are a total masochist, you will want to maintain the high energy and fearless state you plugged into with your early-morning ritual. As daily pressures and doubts begin to seep in, simply give yourself a "fix" of positive energy. All you have to do is repeat your affirmations over and over again until you feel your strength and optimism return. Your Chatterbox will also be trying to enter your consciousness all day; remember to outtalk it. Keep these positive fixes going day and night. Make it a marvelous habit in your life.

9. Before you go to sleep, play or stream a relaxation or meditation track and embrace the soothing messages. *Inner Talk for Peace of Mind* might be a very good choice to send you off to a restful and happy sleep . . . or whatever you like to listen to that gives you a feeling of peace. This is much better than listening to your Chatterbox, which tries to convince you that your life is lacking and that somehow you are not good enough. Awful! Instead, drift off to blissful sleep being fed messages of love and caring. That is far more nourishing for your well-being.

Please believe me when I tell you that if you commit yourself to such a program, your whole world will turn around. Positive thinking changes everything in your life. Without your negative Chatterbox, you will wonder what you were always so afraid of before. You will have energy you never thought possible. You will laugh a lot and love a lot more. You will draw more and more positive people into your life. You will be healthier physically. You will be happy to be alive.

In a short period of time (you'll know when you are ready), you can ease up a bit and begin a maintenance program. Give yourself at least one month, however, before you cut back. If on some days you were not as diligent as you would have liked, *don't* let your Chatterbox scold you. I can just hear it in there, saying, "See, you can't even follow a simple program like this. You'll never feel good. You're hopeless." Just keep remembering that it's only your Chatterbox speaking, and you can outtalk it. "I'm doing it all perfectly!" is a wonderful affirmation when the Chatterbox tries to tell you you've goofed.

I can't stress enough that positive thinking needs daily practice. I've been practicing it for years and still spend some time each day focusing on the elimination of negativity from my thinking. If I stop completely, as I have on occasion, I know my good feelings will slowly diminish. Thank goodness, it is easy to get into the swing of it again simply by following the program. I always ask myself then, "Why do I stop doing something that makes me feel so good?" Stopping the chatter and sending the mind uplifting messages instead is a lifelong task, much like exercising the body. And just as with physical exercise, if you don't use it, you'll lose it.

One more thought about positive thinking: it is important not to use it as an excuse for denial. We begin to feel so good sensing the power of positive thoughts that it is tempting to stifle the sadness and pain that exists, not only in our own lives but in the world as well.

Yes, there is pain in our own lives. We all experience loss and disappointment. No one is immune. And real positive thinking allows the tears to flow . . . always knowing we will get to the other side of the pain and live a beautiful and productive life. Yes, there is pain in the world . . . and real positive thinking allows the tears to flow for the world as well. Starvation exists. Racism exists. Threats of war exist. Environmental problems exist. And on it goes. Let the tears flow, and then get *involved*! Approach your involvement with the positive attitude that something can be done, even if the answer is not readily seen. Denial creates inactivity . . . and so does hopelessness.

No one is immune to pain, and it shouldn't be denied when it exists. The key is to know that you can lead a productive and meaningful life *no matter what the external circumstances are*. What positive thinking does is offer a power boost to help you handle whatever life gives you. Your "bad breaks" do not dominate your life; your indomitable strength does. And when you feel that indomitable strength, you really can handle any of your fears from a position of power—the kind of power that really can make things happen.

6.

When "They" Don't Want You to Grow

The gloom and the fog are beginning to lift. Life is appearing far more manageable now that you have adopted your optimistic attitude. As you begin to put your newfound positiveness into action and make some longed-for changes, you suddenly find that something is amiss with the people in your life. Both inside and outside your home, you begin to realize that some of the significant people in your life don't seem to like the changes in you—even if the old you was a total wreck! What's happening?

What is happening is that others have become accustomed to interacting with you in a certain way, and when that pattern of interaction is broken, there is usually upset of varying degrees. Even when you understand it, this upset can be very disturbing. Not only are you fearful of moving forward, but you are now fearful of losing your relationships. Just when you are in need of a cheering squad, you find yourself faced with enemy troops!

Before I discuss how to deal with family members who are having a hard time with your personal growth, take a good hard look at the people in your life generally. Do they support your growing, or do they drag you down? Do you feel good being around them, or do you feel "infected" by their negativity? Are they excited about the new you that is emerging, or would they prefer the company of the old you that you are outgrowing? If the latter part of all three questions is true, it is time to consider making some changes.

Keep in mind that your goal is to move yourself from pain to power in the way you hold your fear, and remember this:

• • •

**It is amazingly empowering to have
the support of a strong, motivated,
and inspirational group of people.**

• • •

If you are now cringing with the realization that the people in your life belong in the weak, stuck, and depressed category, don't worry. *Awareness* of this fact is the key to the solution. Most of us are *not* aware that we belong to the moan-and-groan crowd until we stop moaning and groaning. When we become aware, things automatically start to take care of themselves.

How? It's quite simple. As you begin to grow, you will notice you no longer want to be around depressing people. Negativity is contagious, and you walk away feeling miserable after spending time in the company of a negative person. Positiveness is conta-gious as well, and spending time with a positive person makes you feel as though you can sprout wings and fly. Soon you'll become discerning. Energy is tangible, and as you become more aware, you will "feel" if a person is positive or negative . . . and you'll be automatically drawn to the more positive. The people in your life are a good indicator of where you are operating on an emotional level. Like attracts like. As you begin to change, you will automat-ically draw and be drawn to a different kind of person.

When this is discussed in my classes, a question that always arises is: "That's all well and good, but what do I do with the old friends I have outgrown?" Many of my students have expressed guilt at the thought of leaving old friends behind. This is under-standable, but totally unwarranted. In the first place, they are as-suming that their old friends are not strong enough to carry on without them. This is a bit presumptuous and more than a bit condescending to their friends. I can guarantee that if you with-draw from their lives, they will find new friends with whom to associate. The Moan and Groan Society will be around for many years to come, and your friends will always find a welcome home there.

There is another possibility: your newfound energy may awaken your friends to new possibilities, and they may join you on your journey toward power, action, and love. That, of course, would be ideal. It is important to remember that, even with your old friends as company, you will want to expand your support system so that you will have all kinds of "advanced" role models to show the way.

What kind of support system am I talking about? The kind that makes you feel *wonderful* about yourself. So that when you say you want to go back to school, or get a new job, or whatever, your friends will say, "I think that is a fantastic idea. You'll do beautifully. Don't worry . . . you have what it takes! Go for it!"

This is the kind of support I'm talking about, instead of "Aren't you taking a big risk? There's so much competition out there, you'll never make it. Why don't you just leave things the way they are?" When you hear that kind of talk, it's time to run the other way.

Among the new friends you make, include those who are farther along the journey than you are at the moment. As Marilyn Ferguson states in her acclaimed book *The Aquarian Conspiracy*:

> *If we are to find our way across troubled waters, we are better served by the company of those who have built bridges, who have moved beyond despair and inertia.*

Although it is a great feeling to be able to lead people to a better place, it is also a relief to be led by others who can show you the way. Life becomes more fun and less of a struggle when you don't have to pioneer on your own. There is a lightness about positive people. They have learned not to take themselves so seriously, and they are a joy to be around. This is not to say that positive thinkers are "flaky." Positive thinkers support people in expanding their own vision into the world to create a healthier planet. When we are concerned with something bigger than ourselves, our fears are greatly diminished. We sense ourselves as being part of a bigger whole—we are not alone and we, perhaps for the first time, are aware of a sense of purpose.

It is incredibly important to your peace of mind and sense of power to have some kind of support group. I can't stress enough how important it is to begin *now* to have strong people in your life, in the form of an established group or simply a group of friends who are consciously in the process of growing. Again, don't worry about your negative friends. It is more than likely that as soon as you stop agreeing with their victim act, they will either fade away or join you on the path to power and love.

How do you begin? Think about people you have recently met and really admire. Do some sleuthing to find out their contact information or locate their social media presence. Email or message them to tell them simply that you were impressed at the first meeting and that you would like to get to know them better. Then invite them to join you for lunch or dinner. I know this can be *very* frightening at first. The first time I did it, many years ago, my hand actually shook as I dialed the phone.

Much to my surprise, the woman I had chosen for my first new friend was thrilled that I had called. At that time my self-esteem was so low, I imagined she would do everything to avoid me. On the contrary—she told me she was really excited I had called. "You are?" was my insecure response. We had a delightful evening together and continue to be good friends today. Initiating relationships became easier for me as time went on, and today I'm blessed with a circle of fantastic friends.

The point is that you must make the effort. So many people sit at home waiting for an invitation and wondering why they are always alone. Nothing is going to come to you—especially in the beginning. You have to go out and create the kind of support system you want. Even if it seems frightening, *do it anyway*! Even if you get a few rejections, keep trying. If you get one good response out of ten, that's great. Remember that people are flattered by your interest, even if for their own reasons they reject your invitation. You will have made them feel good simply by contacting them. Be discriminating in who you approach. Pick someone you perceive as being a few steps ahead of you in personal growth. It will be great for your self-confidence when you eventually find out that you're way ahead of them in many areas. We do tend to greatly underestimate ourselves.

A good place to find such people is at self-improvement classes, workshops, or seminars through your local community centers and colleges. There you will meet people already on the path of personal growth. You will have much in common, and you will likely find more openness with such people.

While it's best if you meet people face-to-face, sometimes you have to start where you are. For most of us, that's in front of a computer screen. There are loads of online courses and seminars that can help you along your path. A quick search will also give you many types of forums, websites, or social media groups that focus on self-improvement and inspiration. A note about meeting people online: when you find a group, chat, or a website that speaks to you, vet it thoroughly before committing your time. The internet is a wonderful place to meet like-minded people, but there are those who spend their time tearing others down rather than building them up. Consider a paid course or workshop to help you find truly like-minded people.

Now that you've got your friends in order, your next question might be *"What do I do when my partner is the one who is dragging me down?"*

This is an important question. It is often our partner who resists our growth most of all. Although we are often shocked and disappointed at this lack of support, it isn't really so surprising. Our partners often perceive that they have much to lose when we begin rocking the boat. It might take a while for them to realize they have more to gain by our growth. The following story is an extreme example of how difficult it is for a partner to accept change—even if that change is from sickness to health.

Whitney

Whitney was one of my earliest students. She lived in Garden City, Long Island, and for eighteen years she had been too frightened to venture any farther. In fact, during the few years prior to her attending my class, she had hardly left her home. She, as you might have guessed, had agoraphobia. My teaching is geared toward everyday fears, as opposed to phobias. Yet something drew her to my course.

In order for her to get there, her husband, Brian, had to drive her into New York City, take her up to the classroom, and wait for her downstairs. She was too frightened to be on her own. When it was her turn to speak in the go-around, I could see the anguish on her face. She was terrified that she was going to have a panic attack.

I used the technique called "paradoxical intention" on Whitney, which, simply stated, means I encouraged her to do the very thing she feared. What we resist, persists. So I told her not to resist and to show us what a panic attack looked like. As predicted, she couldn't muster one up no matter how hard she tried, and ultimately she began to laugh, as did the rest of us. From that moment, she was on her way back to health. She was diligent about doing all the homework assignments, and within a short time she was driving, shopping, and even taking the subway. The class and I watched her transform before our eyes.

One day she came into class a bit disturbed. She said, "As I begin to feel better and better, I'm realizing that my husband is trying to sabotage me. Every time I leave the house, he tries to put all kinds of fear thoughts into my head. When I come home excited about some new thing I've conquered, he withdraws and becomes very aloof. I'm so angry at him! I don't understand what is happening! Why would he do that to me?"

To all of us who have dramatically changed our patterns of relating to people in our lives, the answer was obvious. Brian was doing it for a number of reasons. In the first place, he was threatened by her changes. Before she took the path to recovery, he had a wife who was always waiting for him at home. He never had to concern himself with suspicions of what she might be doing in the outside world. There was tremendous security in that, even though their life was so limited as a result of her phobias.

Second, there was probably actual worry connected with his behavior. For years, she was a little bird in a cage. It was doubtful that any harm would come to her in the confines of their home, but now that she was out in the world, traveling the streets of New York, he was undoubtedly afraid that some harm would come to her. As we worry about our children crossing the street alone for the first time, he worried about his "child," who in many ways was crossing the street for the first time.

Last, her independence was worrying him. For so many years she had desperately needed him to function for her. Now she was functioning on her own. Would she continue to want him if the need was no longer there?

With these thoughts going through Brian's head, no wonder he found it difficult to support Whitney in her growth. As we talked about what he might be feeling, she began to realize that it was *he* who needed the support from her. She admitted that her anger made it hard for her to give him any support. As she put it, "How do you reassure someone when you feel so frustrated, you just want to walk out of the room?"

It took a while, but, happily for Whitney and Brian, they were able to work through the changes that had to take place in order for the marriage to work on a healthier basis. What helped was the fact that Whitney was sure that she would *never* go back to being the pathetic "shut-in" she used to be. If it cost her her husband, so be it! She felt entitled to health after all those years of suffering. It was, therefore, clear to Brian that his manipulations would not work. He understood that either he had to adjust his own behavior or he would lose his wife. His ego was strong enough to overcome his feeling of threat and ultimately he became a tremendous support to Whitney.

Not all relationships are as healthy as those of Whitney and Brian, and change in the unwritten contract of the partnership can signal the end of the relationship. Although the thought that your relationship could break down may be very frightening, in actuality, I know of *no one* who has chosen the path of growth over a relationship who has regretted that choice!

Here are two examples:

Richard

Richard had usually played it safe. He was an accountant who supported his wife and two kids for many years in the same job. In his late 30s, he decided there had to be more to life than he was experiencing. One of the companies for which he had done a great deal of work was for sale. It was a small tech company that showed a great deal of promise. When he discussed the idea of raising the capital and buying the company, his wife couldn't deal with it—her financial security was threatened. Obviously, she had no confidence in his ability to make it work.

Richard decided that for his own mental health, he had to give it a try. He might fail, but if he didn't go ahead with it, he would spend the rest of his life doing what he didn't want to do, which was working for someone else. Despite his wife's disapproval, he made the purchase when he was finally able to raise the capital.

His home situation changed drastically during the process. Naturally, the initial stages of running a new business required a great deal of his time. He experienced nothing but resentment on the part of his wife. He got no support or encouragement from her. He asked her to become involved with him in the company, but she refused.

Their home became a battleground, and when he found himself happy to leave in the morning and unhappy to come home in the evening, he decided it was time to end the relationship. To this day, his ex-wife still considers him selfish and uncaring, simply because he wouldn't play the relationship game according to her rules.

Richard ultimately got a divorce and made a huge success of the business. He grew, and his wife was not able to grow with him. He shudders when he looks back at where he would still be, had he not taken the opportunity that presented itself. His sense of himself has dramatically altered for the better. He felt the fear . . . and did it anyway, even though it meant the breakup of his marriage.

Raquelle

Raquelle also chose growth over an unhealthy relationship. She was married very young and had two daughters in the first four years of her marriage. It did not take long for dissatisfaction to set in, and, with the support of her husband, Roger, she went back to school to complete her education. While initially she was afraid that she had lost her ability to learn after an absence of five years, she was the star in her class and graduated magna cum laude. This success encouraged her to get her master's degree and ultimately her doctorate.

As long as she was a student, things seemed to go well with Roger. He was proud of her, and he really was a marvelous help with the children. But when she finally hung her doctoral diploma on the wall, after many years, her relationship with her husband seemed to change. She was a full-fledged professional with an advanced degree—more advanced than his master's degree. At this point the put-downs began, then the lack of communication, and finally Roger's lateness coming home from work. He began an affair with another woman.

Roger was not able to handle Raquelle's tremendous growth as a human being, and she ended the marriage. It was painful in the beginning—they had been together 12 years—but she began to experience the joy of discovering her own capabilities. She has never regretted her choice to go back to school and create a thriving career.

Her daughters, upset in the beginning, are now very proud of her enormous success. Raquelle serves as an excellent role model for them. She is now married to a man who absolutely adores the fact she is "out there" doing so well. Her aliveness brightens their life, and he loves her for being such an interesting person. He obviously does not feel threatened by her continuing growth.

I know your relationship with your partner is not something to be taken lightly, and it often takes a tremendous amount of courage to risk rocking the boat. It is always a risk, but one I believe to be worth taking. When you choose to remain "stuck" simply because you don't want to upset them, you become resentful of the fact that you have not had your chance to grow. Ultimately, the relationship becomes very strained, and it is not unusual for its breakdown to occur anyway. My suggestion:

• • •

Believe that your partner wants what is best for you and that they will ultimately love the positive changes in you.

• • •

Most probably, your partner will be relieved by your newfound power—it takes some of the responsibility off him or her. Most of us would like to know that the people in our lives are strong, healthy, and loving, instead of needy, weak, and helpless.

Consider this: if your mate turns out to be someone who really prefers you to be needy, weak, and helpless, do you really want to be there?

Not only our partners have a difficult time when we become alive with possibility. Other family members do, too. Children may become pouty, and parents may become judgmental. They, too, may have become accustomed to relating to us in a certain way, and resist our changing.

Children often prey upon a parent's tendencies toward guilt. Parents themselves have their own style. Usually their put-downs are subtle and "sweet," such as, "Darling, are you sure you can do it? You've never been much good at doing things on your own, you know?" or "Darling, you'd better rethink getting a divorce. Nobody wants a woman over 40, especially with two kids" or "You're acting so selfish lately, I hardly recognize you."

Very often parents don't realize they are undermining their children's confidence in themselves, and when this is pointed out to them, they likely will stop the criticism. I once told my mother she obviously had no confidence in me, because she worried about me all the time. She said that was ridiculous; she thought I was the smartest, most competent woman she knew. I pointed out that if that was the case, her worry was unjustified. She looked surprised, and for the first time realized that the way she habitually spoke to me was a carryover from when I was two. It was not based on my current life and lifestyle. From this conversation a miracle happened: she became one of my biggest confidence builders. "You can do it. You can do anything you set your mind to do!" Yes, that's really the way she began speaking to me.

Some may be blessed with a family that is supportive in anything they do, but this is not always the case. Often a great deal of possessiveness is felt by family members, and with that comes a tremendous amount of manipulation. It is important that we learn techniques to create a win-win situation for all parties concerned. This is easier said than done. Behavior change is difficult enough without having to deal with the "crazy" behavior of the people closest to us.

Again I speak from experience. When I went back to college, it seemed that everyone was upset—my mother, my then-husband, my children, and my friends. My mother couldn't understand how I could "leave" my children; my husband resented the fact that I had a life apart from him; my children laid a guilt trip on me when I wasn't there to minister to their every need; and my friends, who were then all housewives and mothers, sided with all of the above! To say that this made me feel insecure about my decision would be an understatement. My reaction was to lash out at anyone who was giving me any difficulty. It was a period of great turmoil. At the time, I was not mature enough to understand why they were upset and to react appropriately. In fact, my inappropriateness was supercharged. I was often really obnoxious. I was acting out what I have subsequently called the PENDULUM SYNDROME, which is illustrated below.

As we strive for Healthy Assertiveness in life, we overshoot the mark in the beginning and swing from Passivity to Aggression many times before we settle into Healthy Assertiveness. More accurately, this swing could be called the PASSIVE-TO-OBNOXIOUS-TO-HEALTHY SYNDROME.

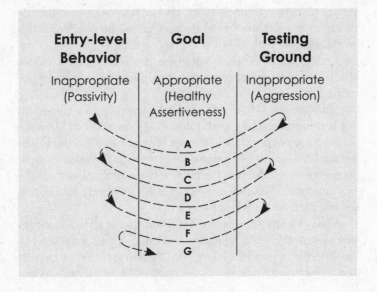

The obnoxious stage can be recognized in the following statements, which are rather mild versions of what came out of my mouth when I was in the throes of the Pendulum Syndrome:

"How dare you!"
"I don't give a damn what you think. I'm doing whatever I please!"
"I don't need you. I never did!"
"You're calling *me* selfish? What about you?"

Although most of us don't like ourselves when we lash out, doing it somehow feels better than reverting to the passive "wimp" we used to be. It is often an understandable part of the process of change. We are not yet sure of ourselves, and our reaction is to defend with all our might.

This swing to Aggression occurs as we hang on to our new behavior for dear life, afraid of reverting to Passivity once again. Yet every once in a while we get scared and do swing back again to a safe place. Hence, the pendulum swings back and forth as we learn the new language of Healthy Assertiveness. We go from Passivity to Aggression many times before we settle into an appropriate range. Ultimately, we do become more comfortable in expressing our needs and doing what we have to do in this world, and we settle down in the appropriate range. But in the beginning, this Pendulum Syndrome is a reality, and it causes much confusion and discomfort, not only for us, but for everyone around us.

Although our behavior is often inappropriate, it is important not to punish ourselves for it. Interestingly, we allow children the leeway they need to test new ways of relating to the world, yet we are hard on ourselves when going through the same process. In reality, we go through fearful new behavioral stages throughout our entire lives, and as we do, we are constantly floundering around until we learn how to do it right.

Again, AWARENESS is the key. Know that in all likelihood, as you start to take risks and grow, you are going to get resistance from people in your life. It's a given. If it isn't your spouse or partner, it will be your parents or your children or your friends. When you rock the boat, someone will tell you to sit down. You need not feel shocked, surprised, or self-righteous. It is their way of defending their security. Often they don't even know they are doing it. In their minds, these admonitions and observations seem totally justified and "for your own good." What is important is that *you* know what is happening.

It will also help if you acknowledge others when they are supporting you. Let them feel good when they are acting in a nurturing way. Send them a loving note expressing your appreciation or some flowers or balloons or whatever will make them happy. This will reinforce the kind of reactions from them you are seeking and will help you focus on their contribution rather than their negativity.

Your awareness of the Pendulum Syndrome should enable you to bypass some of the swings and handle the put-downs more appropriately. There are win-win ways of stopping negative feedback from others. You can learn to respond to significant others in a way that does not demolish them. Here are some examples:

Spouse: "Look at yourself. You've become so selfish since you started that job. Do you really like yourself that way?"

Lose-Lose: "You call me selfish. Who do you think has been taking care of you all these years? Now it's my turn."

Win-Win: "I can see why you think I'm being selfish—I'm not available to you as much as I used to be. All this change is difficult for me as well, but I need to do this for my own growth. If I don't, I know I will hold an awful lot of resentment toward myself and toward you. I really would like to have your support. I know you're feeling a little neglected right now, and it's only natural. I want you to know that I love you very much. What can we do to improve the situation?"

The win-win answer is clear. It states your confidence in yourself (act as if, even if you're not quite sure you *will* make it on your own) and lets your spouse know what you would like from them.

Mom or Dad: "You're always too busy to spend time with me."

Lose-Lose: "I can't be with you 24/7, I've got my own life to live. Stop making everything about you."

Win-Win: "I know I haven't been able to spend much time with you lately and I wish I could visit you more often. My other commitments are demanding more of my time right now, but I am trying my best by calling you several times a week."

Friend: "I feel like you are ignoring me. You never want to hang out anymore."

Lose-Lose: "What's your problem? You can't depend on me all the time to go out and keep you company."

Win-Win: "I know it might seem that way, but right now I'm making room in my life for positive new experiences and relationships—the kind that lift me up and make me a better person. I value our relationship, but right now I need to concentrate on other things."

Children: "You don't care about us anymore."

Lose-Lose: "You kids have no appreciation. I have been responsible for you since the day you were born. Now I do something for myself, and you're complaining!"

Win-Win: "I know it feels different because I'm not around all the time. But I really trust that you guys will find a way to be without me for a few hours. Parents are people, too. And it's important for my peace of mind to be able to work (or go see a movie, or go out with my friends . . .). I will be back later."

The dialogue will not always end there, but that is the tenor of a win-win interaction. An excellent book on the subject of non-aggressive self-defense is *Aikido in Everyday Life* by Terry Dobson and Victor Miller. Their premise is that "the best victory is the one in which everyone wins." It describes a gentle way to win and gives many sample dialogues and reasons why they work.

I suggest you also learn some centering techniques, so that

when you feel yourself swing over to one extreme or the other, you can bring yourself back to a place of balance and harmony. Centering also helps us to resolve conflict. Since there is conflict every day in life, learning to center yourself can be a powerful tool for dealing with conflict in our lives. In my book *End the Struggle and Dance with Life*, I devote a whole chapter to learning about centering. Relaxation audios, meditation, and positive affirmations, as described in the previous chapter, are also a few ways to get yourself to a more peaceful place. Later chapters will offer more tools to gain self-control, so you can have what you want without hurting someone else in the process.

It will greatly help your understanding to know that one of the reasons we react so hostilely when others don't support us is our *need for approval*. Whenever we get upset at the comments of loved ones, it is a clue that we are still acting like a child. Guilt is another clue. Guilt and hostility often mask our anger at ourselves and others for our not being able to break unhealthy ties with loved ones. The lashing-out part of the Pendulum Syndrome comes from this unhealthy attachment.

As you become clearer and more adult about what you need to do in order to grow, loved ones will be able to say anything they please and you won't be affected. You can simply give them a big kiss and say, "I love you but I have to live my own life." End of story. No moans and groans. No hysteria about how badly they are all treating you. In a sense, your need to please shows you what you have to work on—and that is: letting go emotionally of the role of child and stepping into the role of adult. As difficult as it is, cutting childlike relationships with others and substituting more responsible ones allow you to act much more lovingly toward other people in your life. It is a paradox. *The less you need someone's approval, the more you are able to love them.*

Look at people in your life as "practice." The way you react to them allows you to see what you have to work on within yourself. Through them you can practice letting go of inappropriate reactions and developing more responsible ways of behaving. So, instead of wanting to throttle your loved ones when they give you a hard time, it is better to look at them as mirrors of what you still need to work on in terms of your personal growth.

If you cannot reason with loved ones about their destructive behavior toward you, it is best to create some distance until you learn to operate on a more adult level. The father of one of my students, Charlotte, actually used to tell her point-blank that, without a doubt, she was incompetent. No beating around the bush on his part! Eventually, she was able to say to him, "You know, Dad, I love you very much, but until you start respecting who I am, I am going to stay away from you. Right now I need people to support me and love me, and that's not what I feel coming from you." She stayed away from him, making only perfunctory holiday calls, until she felt enough inner strength to handle his put-downs. This was not easy. Saying goodbye to the old relationship with a parent usually requires that we go through grief until the old door is closed and the new one is opened. We are, in effect, grieving for the end of an era. The emerging era, however, brings much more satisfaction with it. Much to Charlotte's surprise, when she finally reconnected with her father, the put-downs stopped.

In all likelihood, prior to her newfound growth, she did present to her father a full-blown picture of incompetence. When that changed, so did his reaction to her. Usually inner strength is respected—we get back what we put out.

The most important thing is for you to be your own best friend. Whatever you are doing—don't put yourself down. Slowly begin to discover which, for you, is the path of the heart. Which path in life will make you grow? That is the path to take. You might be surprised when your loved ones ultimately come to understand and respect that. If not, your new strength will allow you to break unhealthy ties and establish new, healthier ones.

lighten up lighten up lighten up lighten up lighten up lighten up lighten up lighten up lighten up

7.

How to Make a No-Lose Decision

One of the biggest fears that keeps us from moving ahead with our lives is our difficulty in making decisions. As one of my students lamented, "Sometimes I feel like the proverbial donkey between two bales of hay—unable to decide which one I want, and, in the meantime, starving to death." The irony, of course, is that by not choosing, we *are* choosing—to starve. We are choosing to deprive ourselves of what makes life a delicious feast.

The problem is that we have been taught "Be careful! You might make the wrong decision!" A *wrong* decision! Just the sound of that can bring terror to our hearts. We are afraid that the wrong decision will deprive us of something—money, friends, lovers, status, or whatever the *right* decision is supposed to bring us.

Closely tied to this is our panic over making mistakes. For some reason we feel we should be perfect, and forget that we *learn* through our mistakes. Our need to be perfect and our need to control the outcome of events work together to keep us petrified when we think about making a change or attempting a new challenge. No one has ever said that "being perfect" made them happier or feel more fulfilled. In fact, the ideal of being perfect is one of the biggest fabrications that we tell ourselves.

If the statements above describe you, I am going to demonstrate that you are worrying needlessly. There really is nothing to lose, only something to gain, whatever the choices you make or actions you take in life. As I stated earlier, *all you have to do to change your world is change the way you think about it*. This concept works beautifully here. You can actually shift your thinking in such a way as to make a wrong decision or mistake an *impossibility*. Let's begin with decision making.

Suppose you are at a Choice Point in life. If you are like most of us, you have been taught to use the No-Win Model as you think about the decision to be made. The model looks like this:

No-Win Model

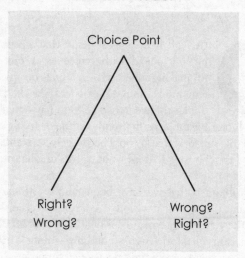

Choice Point

Right?
Wrong?

Wrong?
Right?

Your heart feels heavy about the choice you have to make. You feel somewhat paralyzed as you think about the consequences in life-and-death terms. You stand at the threshold of the decision, lamenting and obsessing: "Should I do this or should I do that? What if I go this way and that happens? What if it doesn't work out the way I plan? What if . . ." The "what ifs" are out in full force. The internal Chatterbox is at it again. You look at the unknown and try to predict the future; you try to take control of outside forces. Both are impossible. At this point you might notice you are driving yourself crazy.

After the decision is made, the No-Win Model makes you constantly reassess the situation, hoping you didn't make a mistake. You keep looking back and berating yourself with "If only I had . . ." You waste valuable energy and you also make yourself miserable.

You gain relief if the outcome is as you hoped it would be—*but* only temporarily. As you breathe a sigh of relief, you are already worrying that the situation might reverse itself and that it might *ultimately* prove to be the wrong decision. Furthermore, you are already fearful about the next decision you have to make, because you will have to go through the whole agonizing process once again. Look familiar? Crazy, isn't it! Clearly, this is a no-win situation. But there is another way—the No-Lose Model.

Go back and stand at the Choice Point again. This time, the situation looks like this:

No-Lose Model

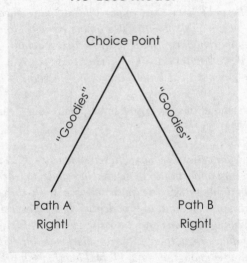

Notice that what lies ahead are simply two paths—A and B— *both of which are right!* Each path has nothing but "goodies" along the way. You are clearly facing a no-lose situation. And what are these goodies? They are opportunities to experience life in a new way, to learn and grow, to find out who you are and who you would really like to be and what you would like to do in this life. Each path is strewn with opportunities—*despite the outcome.* "What? *Despite the outcome?*" Up to this point you may have been willing to go along with me, but those three words are making you a little dubious, if not downright resistant. "What if . . ." comes up again in your thinking. Let me answer your "what ifs" with an example.

Imagine you are faced with the choice of staying with your present job or taking a new one that has opened up for you. If you stand at the No-Win Choice Point, your Chatterbox takes over and craziness begins:

> *"If I stay here I might be missing a very good chance to move ahead. But if I go, maybe I won't be able to handle my new responsibilities. What if I get fired from the new job, and then I have nothing? I really like it here. I'll have more opportunity to move ahead on the new job. Maybe they'll promote me and I'll be making more money. But what if I regret leaving? What if . . . ? Oh, I don't know what to do! I could ruin my whole life if I make the wrong decision!"*

If you stand at the No-Lose Choice Point, your "fearless" self takes over:

> *"Isn't it fantastic! I've been offered a new job. If I take it, I'll have an opportunity to meet new people, to learn new ways of doing things, to experience an entirely different work atmosphere, and to broaden my base of experience. If something happens and it doesn't work out, I know I'll handle it. Even though the job market is difficult right now, I know somehow I'll find another job if I need one. Even that will be an interesting experience, since I'll learn to deal with the loss of a job and learn to solve the problems that might come up if I am unemployed. If I stay, I have an opportunity to deepen the contacts I have made here. I really feel better about myself having been offered the other job, so if I stay, perhaps I'll ask for a promotion. If for some reason it doesn't work out here, there will be other opportunities to pursue. It's all an adventure, no matter which way I turn."*

❀   ❀   ❀

I really do know people who think this way—and their approach to life makes them a joy to be around. They truly live in a no-lose world.

Vernell is a perfect example. Now a practicing psychologist in Los Angeles, he originally intended to follow in his father's footsteps and become a lawyer. His college grades were excellent, and he had no trouble getting into what was considered a fine law school. He studied hard and did very well the first two years. But the time spent away from home began making a difference to his personal priorities. He came to realize that he didn't want to spend the rest of his life in the "combat zone," as he called it, that being a lawyer required. He wanted to help people in a different way, and he decided that clinical psychology was much more in line with his personality. He also realized that part of his decision to be a lawyer was his desire to please his father. But now he was much more in touch with the person inside himself, and he made the decision to leave law school and pursue a career in psychology. His father gave him his blessing but refused to pay any more of his graduate school expenses, thus increasing the difficulty of the decision. But Vernell trusted his gut and withdrew from a situation that did not suit his needs.

Some, including his father, saw those two years at law school as a waste of time, but Vernell never saw it that way. By trying it out, he discovered that being a lawyer was not for him. Finding out what you *don't* like is, paradoxically, as valuable as finding out what you do like. Also, while at law school he made a number of good friends who remain his friends today. And the information he gathered from those first two years has helped him in many personal and professional situations since.

For Vernell, the goodies didn't end there. Since his father had stopped paying his expenses, he had to work for two years to obtain enough money to get started on his degree in psychology. Were those two years wasted? Not at all. His job with a construction company was doubly enriching: he was exposed to a different way of life, and, through one of his coworkers, he met the woman who became his wife. Finally, with a fellowship and his two part-time jobs, Vernell was able to complete his doctorate.

This set of events was invaluable in terms of teaching Vernell to take responsibility for his own life. Perhaps neither he nor his father realized it at the time, but his father really did him a favor by making him stand on his own two feet. Vernell learned that if you want something badly enough, there is a way to get it. And if there was a way, he would find it. He knew that if he hadn't been able to obtain a fellowship, he would have found another way. As a result, he approached future decisions with a feeling of power, energy, and excitement. Remember that underlying all our fears is *a lack of trust in ourselves*. Each step that Vernell took, *despite the outcome*, even when it meant loss of financial support and delay in his education, was an opportunity for him to learn to trust himself to provide for his own needs.

It's interesting to me that when I present the No-Lose Model to my students, the resistance is initially very high. "Oh, come on, you're not being realistic." As I said earlier, we have been taught to believe that negative equals realistic and positive equals unrealistic. When I challenge my students, they can't find more credence in the No-Win Model than in the No-Lose Model, yet the latter can move us from a position of pain to one of power, which is ultimately our goal as we learn to deal with fear. Another point to consider is that it *feels better to come from a no-lose position*. Why continue to resist coming from a no-lose position? Why continue to feel pain, paralysis, and depression? Yet we continue to do it until we incorporate into our being another way of seeing the world. Then we can slowly begin to change the no-win thinking that has kept us victimized.

A critical factor in your accepting the No-Lose Model is the way you think about outcomes and opportunities. It might be hard for you to accept the fact that losing a job is a no-lose situation. Traditionally, opportunities in life are thought of as relating to money, status, and the visible signs of "success." I'm asking you to think of opportunity in an entirely different light. The purpose of this book is to help you handle fear in a way that allows you to fulfill your goals in life. Every time you encounter something that forces you to "handle it," your self-esteem is raised considerably. You learn to trust that you will survive, no matter what happens. And in this way your fears are diminished immeasurably.

• • •

The knowledge that you can handle anything that comes your way is the key to allowing yourself to take healthy, life-affirming risks.

• • •

Getting back to my earlier example, if the outcome of your choosing to move to a new job is for you to lose that job within a few months, you now see how you will have the opportunity to strengthen your self-esteem by facing the storm, regrouping your inner forces, reaching out once again to find a new, perhaps more satisfying position. In the meantime, you will be meeting new people and enlarging your world. Seen in this light, losing your job becomes a no-lose situation.

I have often said to my students that perhaps the "lucky" ones in life are those who have been forced to face things that we all hope we will never have to face—things such as losing a job, the death of a loved one, divorce, bankruptcy, illness. Once you have handled any of those things, you emerge a much stronger person. I know of few people who have experienced loss and haven't felt a large measure of pride in themselves at finding a way to make their lives work despite the adversity. They have discovered that *security is not having things; it's handling things*. Thus, when you can answer all your "what ifs" with "I can handle it," you can approach all things with a no-lose guarantee, and the fear disappears.

Now that you've learned there really are no right or wrong decisions when using the No-Lose Model, there are steps you can take to heighten your awareness about the alternatives that lie before you. This awareness will better improve the chances of the outcome being aligned with your wishes, and it will give you greater peace of mind. I suggest that the following steps be taken when you face a major decision and after you've made one.

BEFORE MAKING A DECISION

1. *Focus immediately on the No-Lose Model.* Affirm to yourself, "I can't lose—regardless of the outcome of the decision I make. The world is a place for opportunity, and I look forward to the opportunities for learning and growing that either pathway gives me." Push out thoughts of what you can lose, and allow only thoughts of what can be gained. Use the exercises in the chapter on positive thinking.

2. *Do your homework.* There is much to learn about the alternatives that lie before you. It is most helpful to talk to as many people as will listen. Don't be afraid to approach professionals relative to the decision to be made. A few might put you off, but most will be happy to help. In fact, they will be flattered that you came to them for advice.

Look for feedback from other sources as well. Talk to people in a coffee shop, the barbershop or hair salon, the doctor's office, or wherever. Instead of checking your email on your phone while waiting in line, why not turn to the person behind you and start a conversation? People you meet in unlikely places can create a valuable connection for you in ways you never could have imagined, or they might give you an insight learned from their personal experiences.

It is important that you talk to the "right" people. Let me give you my definition of the right people. They are those who support your learning and growing. If you talk to people who constantly put down the possibilities open to you, they are the wrong people to talk to. Politely say thank you and go on to someone else. You don't have to continue having conversations about your decision with those who make you feel bad about yourself. You should talk to people who can support you with statements like "I think it's terrific you're considering . . ." or "I think you'll do beautifully at . . ." or "I think you'll be a success at whatever you choose." You get the picture. Why put yourself in a position to feel miserable when it's so easy to feel great?

Also, don't hesitate to talk about your plans just because you are fearful that if they don't work out, you'll look like a "failure."

Swallow your pride. By not investigating as fully as you can, you are cutting off valuable sources of information that might help you enormously. Remember:

· · ·

**You're not a failure if you don't make it;
you're a success because you try.**

· · ·

One of my students was concerned about being called a "talker" rather than a "doer" if she made too many false starts. There is no such thing as a false start if you are seriously committed to advancement. My first experience in the publishing world serves as a good example.

Years ago, I made the decision to publish a book of poems I had written. Since I knew nothing about the publishing world, I started talking to as many people as I could about how I should best proceed. I took a course on getting published; I called strangers who worked in various publishing houses (and was surprised that they were most anxious to help); I submitted my book to about 20 publishers and received one rejection after another. But I just kept talking about my career as a writer. I'm sure there were those who said, "Who's she kidding? It will never happen." But I made up my mind. I kept telling myself, "I will be a successful author. In the face of everyone telling me that authors don't make money or it's impossible to get a book published, I know I will. I know I will have a loving impact on many people's lives. I know I have a very definite purpose, and I am opening up all of my channels of receptivity so that I can follow my heart."

Over lunch one day, Ellen Carr, a business associate and now a dear friend, and I decided to write and self-publish a short guidebook for women about getting a job. We were concerned about the number of talented women we knew whose fears of rejection and failure kept them from even trying to enter the job market. Again I started talking about our project to everyone I knew, and again a whole series of delays occurred that made some people doubt that the book would ever be published. But I just kept talking, as did Ellen, and we found ourselves meeting all sorts of interesting people who were invaluable in helping us with our project. And that joyous day did arrive when our books were finally delivered to us.

It could be said that there were many false starts in my writing career. Not so! Each step along the way made me more and more ready to enter the field, even though the outcome may not have been in the form originally pictured. And I certainly learned how to deal with rejection! Putting your ideas out into the world by constantly talking about them may create a few doubters, yet not only does talking bring valuable information, *it clarifies your intention to have it happen*! Intention is a powerful tool in creating what you want in your life.

3. *Establish your priorities.* This will require some soul-searching. Give yourself time to really think about what you want out of life. This is a very difficult thing to discover for most of us, since we are trained at an early age to do what other people want us to do. We are out of touch with those things that really bring us satisfaction. To make it easier, ask yourself which pathway is more in line with your overall goals in life—at the present time.

It is important to remember that goals constantly change as you go through life, and you have to keep reassessing them. The decision you make today might not be the decision you would make five years from now, or would have made five years ago. If you are having trouble clarifying your overall goals, don't worry about it. It may take many more decisions and much more experimentation with different situations to discover how best to order your priorities. At least you are beginning to pay attention to who you are. Allow yourself confusion in the searching process. It is through confusion that you finally come to clarity.

4. *Trust your impulses.* Although you might have difficulty getting to the "person within" through the soul-searching process, your body sometimes gives some good clues about which way to go. Even after you've done your homework, talked to many people, and come up with a logical choice, it is possible that your impulse is telling you to go with the other choice. Don't be afraid to trust it. Very often your subconscious mind sends knowing messages as to which choice is better at a particular time. As you start paying attention to your impulses, you will be surprised at the good advice you are giving yourself.

I was surprised when I "trusted my gut" and found a new career. My intention after getting my doctorate in psychology was to ultimately set up a private practice. A few months after I began treating patients in a mental-health clinic, the opportunity opened for me to help a friend who had become executive director of a marvelous health facility called "The Floating Hospital, New York's Ship of Health." (The Floating Hospital at the time was a ship that sailed around Manhattan delivering health-care services to the underserved but has now transitioned to a land-based service.) My instinct told me to take the job even though it didn't logically fit into the plans I had made for myself. Something within me said, "Go for it."

Within months, my friend resigned, and I was made executive director. Nowhere in my plan was it written that I would become an administrator. Previously, I had viewed myself as a follower, not a leader, and the whole concept of being at the helm had never entered my mind. Somehow my subconscious knew I could handle it and pushed me to take the job. "What am I doing here?" I asked myself as I went through fear and uncertainty in handling the demands of the position. But as I learned and grew with the job, I realized I loved administrative work and, in fact, became very capable in that area. In addition, the Floating Hospital brought me rich, wonderful, crazy, hilarious, poignant, and exciting experiences and challenges that I never thought would be possible for me. But my subconscious mind had known. It had overridden my conscious, logical mind, which had said, "Don't deviate from your plan" and "You can't handle this job."

I must make it clear, following the concept that there is no such thing as a wrong decision, that if I had chosen to remain a therapist in the mental-health clinic, *that choice also would have brought me rich opportunities for experiencing life in a new and different way*. There was no right or wrong decision, just different ones.

5. *Lighten up.* We live in a world where most people take themselves and their decisions very seriously. I have news for you. Nothing is *that* important. Honestly! If as a result of a decision you make, you lose some money, no problem—you learn to deal with losing money. If you lose a lover, no problem—you find another one. If you choose to divorce, no problem—you learn to handle living on your own. If you choose to marry, no problem—you learn to handle a new kind of sharing.

I may make it sound easy, but it is something I have to work on constantly. To remind me, I have sitting on my desk a pink-quartz statue of the Laughing Buddha. There is a look of pure joy on his face, and he appears to be having a big belly laugh. The Laughing Buddha is so happy because he knows that everything is all right. He knows that whatever decision he makes, it really doesn't matter. He knows that the result of any decision can be wondrous. Because of this, he feels free, safe, and complete. I like to look at my Laughing Buddha, for he reminds me that I shouldn't take things too seriously, especially myself. I might never get to the point of pure happiness that he has obtained, but just looking at his face every morning points me in the right direction.

Start thinking about yourself as a lifetime student at a large university. Your curriculum is your total relationship with the world you live in, from the moment you're born to the moment you die. Each experience is a valuable lesson to be learned. If you choose Path A, you will learn one set of lessons. If you choose Path B, you will learn a different set of lessons. Geology or geometry—just a different teacher and different books to read, different homework to do, different exams to take. *It really doesn't matter.* If you take Path A, you get to taste strawberries. If you take Path B, you get to taste blueberries. If you dislike both strawberries and blueberries, you can find another path. The trick is simply to make whatever place you're in your educational forum and learn everything you can about yourself and the world around you. So—*lighten up!* Whatever happens as a result of your decision, *you'll handle it!*

AFTER MAKING A DECISION

1. *Throw away your picture.* We all create expectations of what we would like to have happen after a decision is made. The picture in our mind's eye might have served a valuable function in helping to make a decision. But once the decision is made, let the picture go. The mental picture you created represented your hopes at the time. Since you can't control the future, the picture can create unhappiness if your hopes are dashed. Disappointment may make you miss the good that can come out of every situation in which you find yourself. Don't forget to look for that silver lining. If you see the outcome of a decision as looking a certain way, you will increase the likelihood of missing other opportunities. Yet the unexpected opportunities can create more of value than your original picture. If you are focused on "the way it's supposed to be," you might miss the opportunity to enjoy the way it is or to have it be wonderful in a totally different way from what you imagined.

To help erase your mental picture, try an exercise from my book *Embracing Uncertainty*. The "I Wonder . . ." exercise on the following page, adapted for Making a No-Lose Decision, teaches us to create a "wondering life" instead of a "hoping life." Wondering is the opposite of getting our hopes up. Hoping makes us uneasy, since we are invested in a particular outcome, yet wondering makes us curious and open to whatever happens.

2. *Accept total responsibility for your decisions.* This is a tough one! We all have a tendency to look around for someone to blame if things are not working out to our liking. I really hated my stockbroker when the stock he recommended went down instead of up. It took great fortitude to admit to myself, "I made the decision to buy. No one twisted my arm." I lamented until I created an "opportunity" from my ill-fated decision. What did I learn? A lot! I learned I had to find out more about the stock market, instead of relying totally on my stockbroker's opinion. I learned that I was terribly insecure about money and had to work on that. I learned I could lose money in the stock market and yet life went on just as it did before. I learned that if in the future I

I Wonder . . .

Take a blank sheet of paper or open a clean document on your computer or mobile phone. Draw a line down the center. On the left side make a list of hopes you have regarding your decision. For example, if you have decided to apply for a promotion, write:

> *I hope I'll get promoted.*
> *I hope I'll get a raise.*
> *I hope my friends will be impressed.*
> *I hope I'll do a great job.*

Write down as many hopes as you can think of associated with your decision. Once you've written down all you can, on the right side replace the words "I hope" with the words "I wonder if."

> *I wonder if I'll get promoted.*
> *I wonder if I'll get a raise.*
> *I wonder if my friends will be impressed.*
> *I wonder if I'll do a great job.*

See how the pressure of the decision is relieved when we live in wonder instead of hope? With this exercise you can change your mental picture from something uncertain to something empowering.

lost money on the stock market, it wouldn't be such a big deal, and that stocks can go up again, as mine did eight months later. When looked at in that light, it wasn't a bad decision after all. When you can find the *opportunity* in any decision, it is much easier to accept the *responsibility* for making it.

When you take responsibility for your decisions, you become

a lot less angry at the world and, most important, a lot less angry at yourself!

3. *Don't protect, correct.* It is most important to commit yourself to any decision you make and give it all you've got. But if it doesn't work out, *change it*! Many of us are so invested in making the "right" decision that even if we find we don't like the path we have chosen, we hang in there for dear life. To my way of thinking, this is the height of craziness. There is tremendous value in learning you *don't* like something. Then it is simply a matter of changing your path. Yes, there are those who keep flitting from place to place, using "change it" as an excuse for noncommitment. I'm not talking about that, and you'll know the difference within yourself. If you've truly committed yourself to something, given it everything you've got, and then if you conclude that it is not for you—move on to something else that might be right for you.

When you decide to change paths, you will often face criticism from those around you. "What do you mean you want to change your career? You've invested five years in building up your dental practice! All that time and money down the drain!" Explain that none of it has been a waste. At one time it was the right thing for you to do. Much was learned and much was gained in the way of experience. It simply doesn't feel right anymore—it's time to change. I know many people who stay locked in unsatisfactory situations that no longer work for them because they've invested so much time and energy and it would be a shame not to continue. How illogical! Why invest more if it's no longer paying off? Remember—the quality of your life is at stake!

In his book *Actualizations*, Stewart Emery presents an excellent model for changing your direction in life. He learned it while seated on the flight deck of an airplane on the way to Honolulu. He noticed a console, which was identified by the pilot as the inertial guidance system. The purpose of the system was to get the plane within one thousand yards of the runway in Hawaii within five minutes of the estimated arrival time. Each time the plane strayed off course, the system corrected it. The pilot explained that they would arrive in Hawaii on time in spite of "*having been in error 90 percent of the time.*" Emery takes it from there, stating: "So the path from here to where we want to be starts with an error, which we correct, which becomes the next error, which we correct and that becomes the next error, which we correct. So the only time we are truly on course is that moment in the zigzag when we actually cross the true path." From the analogy, we see that the trick in life is not to worry about making a wrong decision; *it's learning when to correct*! My concept of the model looks like this:

Off Course/Correct Model

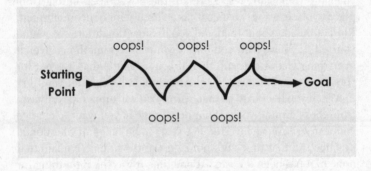

There are many inner clues that help you know when it is time to correct. The two most obvious are confusion and dissatisfaction. Ironically, these are considered negatives, instead of positives. I know it is hard to accept, but *an upset in your life is beneficial*, in that it tells you that you are off course in some way and you need to find your way back to your particular path of clarity once again. Your confusion and dissatisfaction are telling you that you're off track, and, as the Chinese proverb says, "If you don't change your direction, you're likely to end up where you're heading."

Physical pain is easily seen as beneficial, even though it can be very uncomfortable. It is an obvious symptom that something is wrong with your body. A pain in your right side might save your life by signaling an appendicitis attack. If you don't pay attention to it, you could die. Mental pain is just as much a "blessing," because it is telling you that something is wrong with the way your life is going. It is a sign that something needs attention and correction—whether it is the way you think about the world or what you are doing in the world—or both. The pain is simply saying, "Hey, that's not it!"

The way to figure out how to get back on course is through the exploration process—reaching out through self-help books, workshops, friends, support groups, therapy, or whatever seems right for you when you reach out for help. As long as you are open to reaching out, help will be there. Remember, "When the student is ready, the teacher will appear." You will never be ready if you are busy protecting the course you have chosen for yourself. You will be perpetually off course and never reach your destination. When you are constantly aware of the clues that signal "time to correct," you will always end up in the right spot—or at least in the vicinity.

As a handy review, below is a summary of the steps in the decision-making process. By applying these, you'll breathe a lot easier as you make choices throughout your lifetime.

NO-LOSE DECISION-MAKING PROCESS

Before Making a Decision

1. Focus on the No-Lose Model.
2. Do your homework.
3. Establish your priorities.
4. Trust your impulses.
5. Lighten up.

After Making a Decision

1. Throw away your picture.
2. Accept total responsibility.
3. Don't protect, correct.

If you don't think the above makes absolute sense, let me summarize the steps we usually take when using the No-Win Model:

NO-WIN DECISION-MAKING PROCESS

Before Making a Decision

1. Focus on the No-Win Model.
2. Listen to your mind drive you crazy.
3. Paralyze yourself with anxiety as you try to predict the future.
4. Don't trust your impulses—listen to what everyone else thinks.
5. Feel the heaviness of having to make a decision.

After Making a Decision

1. Create anxiety by trying to control the outcome.
2. Blame someone else if it doesn't work out as you pictured.
3. If it does work out, keep wondering if it would have been better the other way.
4. Don't correct if the decision is "wrong"—you have too much invested.

Does this last summary sound painfully (and comically) familiar? Yes, we certainly do know how to drive ourselves crazy!

Now that I've demonstrated the No-Win and No-Lose Models as they pertain to decision making, I trust you can see how it is impossible to make a mistake. Just as each decision is an opportunity to learn, each "mistake" is also an opportunity to learn, rendering it impossible to make a mistake. A great researcher, having "failed" 200 times before he found the answer to one of his burning questions, was asked, "Doesn't it bother you that you failed all those times?" His answer was, "I never failed! I discovered 200 ways *not* to do something!"

After much consideration, I have come to the conclusion that if you haven't made any mistakes lately, you must be doing something wrong. You'll never get to Hawaii! You haven't even left the airport yet! You've never even gotten off the ground! You are taking no risks—nor are you enjoying the "goodies" life has to offer. What a waste!

I remember a time in my life when I was frightened of just about everything—fearful that I would fail in all my attempts to fulfill my dreams. So I just stayed home, a victim of all my insecurities. I'd like to report that it was an ancient Zen master who snapped me back into awareness. But it wasn't. It was actually an airline commercial that used the slogan "Get into this world." When I saw the commercial, I suddenly realized that I had stopped participating in the world. With this "enlightenment," I started pushing myself out there once again. I realized I had to shift from being afraid of making a mistake to being afraid of *not* making a mistake. If I am not making any mistakes, I can be sure I sure I am not learning and growing.

When you consider that mistakes are an integral part of living, it is amazing how we are taught to think we must be perfect. This "mistake" in our thinking, that we must try to be perfect, has created many fears about being adventurous and trying out new territories. Let's take an example from a favorite national pastime, baseball. It is extremely rare for a baseball player to attain a .400 average. In fact, most players barely average .300. Translated, .400 means having a hit four times out of ten at bat—four successes out of ten tries. That's a champion's performance—and yet it falls short of perfect—and most of us are just beginners!

You are not going to succeed in everything you attempt in life. That's guaranteed. In fact, the more you do in life, the more chance there is not to succeed in some things. Look at how rich your life can be, however, from your many adventures. Win or lose, you just keep winning! Using the Off Course/Correct Model, you can now have a new freedom in living life fully.

Although you now know how to minimize your fears about decision making and making a mistake, you might notice that adopting the concepts presented is more difficult than it sounds. Again I remind you of the lengthy process involved in behavior change. *Simply begin*! Keep working on it. Keep reinforcing the new way of thinking presented here by using the exercises below to help you push through your fears about making decisions or mistakes.

Are you making any mistakes lately? I hope so!

EXERCISES

1. Using the No-Lose Model, consider some decisions you are now facing. Write down all the positive things that can happen by using either pathway—even if the outcome might not be what you picture.

2. Learn the concept IT DOESN'T REALLY MATTER by starting with little decisions you face each day. As you ponder which suit to wear to the office, notice that it doesn't really matter; which restaurant to eat at tonight, it doesn't really matter; which movie to see, it doesn't really matter. Each choice simply produces a different experience. Slowly you will be able to apply this concept to larger and larger decisions. Put signs in your home and office that say:

IT REALLY DOESN'T MATTER

to remind yourself when you are being needlessly obsessive.

3. Also, put signs in your home and workplace that say:

SO WHAT! I'LL HANDLE IT!

If things don't work out the way you want, so what! What's the big deal, anyway? This reminder will help you lighten up about life as you learn you can handle whatever happens after you've made your decision.

4. Look at clues in your life that suggest you are off course, and begin making your game plan to correct the situation. Feelings of confusion, doubt, dissatisfaction, and even annoyance are good indicators that you are off course. No decision you make has to remain permanent. Remember that no experience is wasted. Learning what you don't want is as important as knowing what you do want.

8.

How Whole Is Your "Whole Life"?

"I am devastated without Ryan. He was my whole life!" Kyle was one of my students whose husband had just divorced him after five years of marriage. He wasn't kidding when he said that Ryan was his whole life, for that's exactly what he had made him. Nothing and no one else had any real significance.

This, of course, explains Kyle's devastation and desperate sense of emptiness when Ryan left. It probably also explains, in part, the breakdown of the marriage. As I explain in *The Feel the Fear Guide to Lasting Love*, dependency in a relationship creates some very unattractive side effects—anger, jealousy, resentment, clinging, nagging—all very unpleasant to live with. These self-defeating qualities are the result of a deep-seated fear of losing what we see as the basis of our entire identity.

Matthew, a public-relations executive, chose to create his identity in the area of work. For him, there was only his career; nothing else mattered. As with Kyle, negative side effects accompanied his emotional dependency. At work, he was protective instead of expansive and giving; he usurped credit for everything, ignoring the contributions of those with whom he worked; and in his constant attempt to gain approval from his superiors, he never took a chance. Thus his creativity was greatly diminished.

When Matthew lost his job due to a series of cutbacks, he predictably experienced a feeling of devastation, an extreme sense of helplessness, and thoughts of suicide—all brought on by a horrible feeling of emptiness. His lifeline had been severed.

People who have lived their entire adult years emotionally tied to their work often fall apart when they are forced to retire. It is as though their lives are over—in fact, many get ill or die soon after their retirement begins. How sad that they cannot enjoy what is potentially the most enjoyable and creative part of their lives!

Since high school, Hannah has been the queen of social media. She counts thousands of followers on Instagram, Twitter, and other platforms. She loves the feedback—getting hundreds of "likes" every time she posts a photo. Her college experience was more successful online than it was in real life, but she managed to graduate. A few months after college, she got a good job working for a media company when suddenly her life fell flat.

She couldn't spend as much time posting to her accounts as she had, so her followers were falling away. On top of that, none of her co-workers were impressed with her social media fame. In fact, many of them had more followers than she did. After feeling like the center of attention for years, she suddenly felt like a nobody. Talk about living a one-dimensional life! Hannah had put all her effort into one part of her life, and when it was eliminated, she was completely deflated. She was depressed because she had to start again from nothing.

Zahara, a mom, made her *children* the totality of her life. To those who didn't understand, she looked like, and believed herself to be, a "good" mother. She was always there when the children came home from school, she catered to their every need, and she prided herself on the fact that her children always came first.

If Zahara had been more honest with herself, she would have seen she was using her children to create her reason to exist. Those who really knew her were aware of the inevitable side effects—a need to dominate, overprotectiveness, and self-righteousness. This mirrored the total emptiness she felt inside. Staying home with children is not necessarily a bad choice, but when parents depend on children for their own emotional survival, it is clearly detrimental. Not only is it unhealthy for the parent; it is also unhealthy for the children. A parent's dependency is a heavy burden for a child to bear!

The underlying feeling that Kyle, Matthew, Hannah, and Zahara shared was an extreme sense of neediness. When they lost the things in their lives to which they were emotionally tied, this neediness was exposed. I will wager that most of you, at some time or another, have experienced this same kind of neediness. If so, you will agree it is one of the most painful feelings you can experience. And to make matters worse, when you are in the throes of desperation, there seems to be little you can do to make yourself feel better.

This raises a question: is there anything that can be done to help loosen the grip of this intense neediness, that can make us feel whole despite a great loss in our life? If there is, imagine how greatly our fear of loss could be diminished. The answer to this question is undeniably YES! That should come as a relief.

Although you should be ecstatic that relief is possible, it is important to keep in mind that, as with everything else associated with change, it takes a great deal of awareness, patience, and perseverance to break strong emotion-backed patterns. This should not worry you. While it may sound like an unpleasant task, it really isn't, *if* you take it in small and manageable steps and allow yourself time really to enjoy the process.

So I invite you to try an alternative way of handling your life; it is geared toward helping you release the desperation, emptiness, and fear that may be attached to certain aspects of your life. I know from my own experience that this release is possible. This chapter spells out the steps necessary for change. I promise you these steps offer some interesting insights. Yet only through action and commitment can they become powerful tools that will absolutely change the quality of your life.

It will be helpful first for you to understand more clearly what I consider to be the cause of the emptiness you feel when your life is out of balance. Using RELATIONSHIP as an example, the following box illustrates what your Whole Life looks like when you focus emotionally on only one area:

Whole Life with Relationship

Relationship

If, as in Kyle's case, the big R disappears, life suddenly looks like this:

Whole Life Without Relationship

No wonder you feel empty! No wonder you have the urge to replace that relationship immediately! There's nothing left!

It doesn't have to be this way. Look at the following Whole Life, which represents an entirely different way of seeing things. Not only is Megan's grid filled with nourishment and aliveness, but the entire area of her Life seems to have increased, which, in effect, gives her more for her money. Let's assume that Megan, too, experiences the loss of her love. What does her Whole Life look like then?

Whole Life with Relationship

Contribution	Hobby	Leisure
Family	Alone Time	Personal Growth
Work	Relationship	Friends

What a difference compared with Kyle's loss! You will notice from the grid that the loss of Megan's relationship leaves a hole. But it hardly wipes her out! Yes, there was pain when Megan split from her partner; yes, she is lonely at times; and yes, she would like eventually to have a successful relationship. Yet, without it, her life still works beautifully. Each day is filled with a multitude of experiences from the other parts of her life that bring her joy and satisfaction; hence, her neediness is gone. There are so many resources available to her that she truly feels as if life is a giant cornucopia that will never be empty.

Whole Life Without Relationship

Contribution	Hobby	Leisure
Family	Alone Time	Personal Growth
Work		Friends

At this point in one of my classes a student piped up to say that she, too, has many things in her life—family, children, job, friends—but the only thing that *means* anything to her is her relationship. I pointed out that this is where the awareness, perseverance, and patience come in—to enhance the *commitment* she has to each area of her life.

Commitment, as I am using the term, means consciously giving 100%—everything you've got—to each "box" of the grid. For example, when you are at work, work full out, holding nothing back; when you are with your family, consciously be *with* them, 100%; when you are with friends, be there 100% . . . and so on.

As I started explaining commitment to my class, Sandy, another student, immediately responded that her job was only temporary, until she found something better. In the meantime, she was bored out of her mind and couldn't wait to leave it. Therefore, how could she possibly commit herself to being there 100%? I explained that commitment doesn't mean it has to last forever, but *while you are there* commit yourself 100%. By doing this, the quality of your life and those around you will improve 100%.

I gave her a tool to use on the job to enhance the concept of commitment. This tool is to *"act as if" you really count*. What would that look like? What would she be doing if she knew she really counted? Some possibilities the class came up with were creating daily goals and seeing that they are completed, interacting with other staff members in a way that would make their day happier, creating an environment that is a pleasure to work in. She added, "I would also get there on time." Sandy promised she would give it a try after I assured her that committing herself to this job would not mean that she would be there forever.

Sandy returned to class the following week very excited about what had transpired. We were all struck by the increased level of her energy. She reported that she had taken a plant and a poster to work, which immediately brightened her little area. She was complimentary and helpful to the people around her, and each night before she left the office she created goals to complete the following day. As each day progressed, she focused on her goals and was amazed to find she now got twice as much done each day. She got hooked on the act of checking off her goals—it felt so good. When on the rare occasion she didn't get to something on the list, she merely carried it over to the next day.

Sandy was amazed at the response. One of her coworkers actually asked her what she was on, and said, "Whatever it is, continue taking it!" But the magical result was that *she actually began to enjoy her job*. Participating 100% eliminates boredom. Once Sandy got over her "woe is me" attitude and began to choose to be there 100%, a feeling of satisfaction resulted. Her "acting as if" she counts creates other benefits as well: increased self-esteem, a good reference when she finally does move on to another job, and the realization that she actually can make a difference. This, of course, makes her feel more powerful in a world where so many people feel helpless.

To make commitment a less heavy concept, keep in mind that, contrary to what we have been taught, it doesn't necessarily mean forever.

For example, my job as the executive director of the Floating Hospital brought me a great deal of joy and satisfaction, but after eight years I began to feel I was ready for another kind of challenge. Since I was totally committed to the Floating Hospital, I was determined that it would operate just as smoothly after my departure as before. I began breaking in someone to replace me. I began delegating more and more. I gradually familiarized the board of trustees with the new person I thought would be perfect for the job. I prepared everyone for my leaving. So you see that, even though I was on my way out, I was committed to that job 100%.

At the same time, I was totally committed to having my life work after I left my job. In my free hours, I began teaching, writing, and increasing my private psychotherapy practice. In two years, the groundwork had been laid for the future of both the Floating Hospital and my new career. I was ready to leave.

The same principle works in the area of relationship. No one really knows how long any given relationship will last. But until you decide to let it go, it is important that you give your partner and yourself the respect and dignity you both deserve by committing yourself to be there 100%. If the day arises when you know that it is time to split, you will know that you gave it everything you had. And if, for some reason, your partner decides to end the relationship, you will know you did your best. There is nothing to regret. If you have already incorporated the grid concept into your life, the loss will not be enormous, since you have so many other areas of nourishment in your life.

One area of the grid needs some explanation: the area of CONTRIBUTION. This is the area that allows you to make your own special difference in the world. Contribution is discussed in a later chapter; for now, simply note that it is from the area of contribution that much of your self-esteem and satisfaction in life can come. To know that you can make a difference in this world means that you are not helpless, that you are a meaningful force in the world.

It is important that you don't think of contribution in such grand terms as those of Mohandas Gandhi, Martin Luther King Jr., Nelson Mandela, or Albert Einstein. Contribution in the way that I am using it means beginning exactly where you are, looking around, seeing what needs to be done, and doing it. This could relate to your family, your friends, your community, your country, the world. There is not a person alive who is not capable of greatly contributing to the well-being of this planet. Just changing your attitude can affect the world around you.

Now that you understand the concept of the grid and recognize its importance in reducing many of your fears regarding relationship, job, children, and so on, you are ready to take steps to incorporate this powerful tool into your daily life.

Here are the steps:

1. Simply recognize that you might be caught in a vicious circle. If you look carefully at your past, you will probably notice that every time negative feelings associated with loss came up, you took the very same pathway to try to relieve the discomfort: you tried to re-create what you had lost.

For example, what's the first thing many of us do when we

are devastated by the loss of a relationship? We simply substitute names. And when the next love of our life leaves, we experience the same feeling of devastation. Then what do we do? It's not hard to guess—we go out and find another "one and only" without whom we would simply die!

If this or a similar pattern sounds familiar, it is important not to make a big thing out of it. Just recognize that up until now you simply did not have an appropriate framework within which to create a healthier way to act. The mere fact that you acknowledge the possibility of another way is enough to get you to the next step.

2. Create your own Whole Life Grid. Begin by making a nine-box square like the one below.

Personal Whole Life

Take some time to think about what components you would like to include in your life and begin filling in the boxes. I am a great believer in setting the stage whenever I begin any kind of introspection, so I recommend that you play some calming music in the background while you are filling in the boxes. Make sure you are alone and that your phone is turned off.

3. After you have filled in your grid, pick one of the boxes to work on. Shut your eyes and visualize what you would like that part of your life to look like. What would you be doing? How would you be interacting with the people around you? How would it feel? Remember the two key ingredients: 100% commitment and acting as if you count. Let's call them the MAGIC DUO, for that's exactly what they create in your life—magic.

4. When you get a clear picture, take a blank piece of paper and begin writing down what your mind created for you, paying attention to all the details. This will help you with Step 5.

5. List the many things that would have to be done in order to make your visualization become a reality. Again, take time to think this through carefully. I cannot repeat it too frequently:

. . .

Action is the key to your success.

. . .

You have to *do* something to make your real life match your visualization. So your actions are critical.

Let's see how this might actually work. If you had picked the area of PERSONAL GROWTH, you might see yourself taking classes and workshops, reading books and attending lectures. In your visualization, the Magic Duo assures that you will approach all of this with a will that keeps you focused, and also assures your active participation at all times.

If you are in a workshop or online course, you might see yourself interacting with the other students, doing all the homework, whether it is a credit course or not, happily anticipating the next class, and feeling really happy that you have chosen to be there.

By the way, when you take this concept into the real world, old habits will emerge—that's a given! Thus, when you are actually at a workshop or online course, you might suddenly be overcome by thoughts about what you are obsessed with—your job, your ex, whatever it is that has taken over your life. In the beginning, your mind *will definitely, without question*, want to pull you out of your commitment, and it will take your constant vigilance to control the wandering. Eventually you will be able to say, "To heck with it—I'm here to learn!" Eventually you will be able to make your mind focus on the matter at hand and take in what is happening around you. And then guess what happens! The neediness begins to disappear. Imagine what this does for your self-esteem! The problem with needy people is that they can't take in anything around them. Then they wonder why they are starving emotionally.

What about the area of FRIENDS? What would that look like? Here, you might see yourself inviting them over for dinner, creating a terrific evening out, sending them a greeting card of appreciation, or simply calling or texting them to tell them you were thinking about them. In the real world, when with your friends you will probably be distracted by your ex or some other preoccupation. This is the time to call in the Magic Duo. Begin by focusing on your commitment to be a wonderful friend, "acting as if" you truly make a difference in your friends' lives. From that mental place, you will begin to find much pleasure and fulfillment.

When I was a young woman, my friends and I had an unwritten contract: "I'll keep my date with you as long as Mr. Wonderful doesn't call." Although everyone seemed to have understood the rule, looking back I consider it a lousy policy—stupid, as well, since I always had such a great time with my girlfriends. As I matured I stopped treating my friends with such disrespect. An interesting side effect was that I ceased being considered a last-minute date by the male population. The men in my life began phoning days and sometimes weeks in advance when they knew I would not cancel other commitments to be with them.

Let's look at the area of LEISURE. This one stumps a lot of my students, and I admit it is an area I must work on daily. Many of us tend to be achievement-oriented and get anxious when taking time to relax and enjoy ourselves. It's hard to find the balance in our lives. It seems to be okay when you're relaxing with your partner or friends, but when on your own, you feel you should be accomplishing something. Again, the way to release this anxiety is to call upon the Magic Duo. By committing yourself 100% to your relaxation and "acting as if" your well-being counts, you can enjoy taking some time alone for yourself.

To help myself out, I've created the concept of the "holi-hour," a shortened version of the holi-day. I allow myself at least an hour each day to relax totally. It could mean reading magazines, walking on the beach, or shopping. This helps greatly in keeping me refreshed in my work. Very often I get some of my best ideas during leisure time, when my mind is not so cluttered.

6. Do Steps 3, 4, and 5 for every area of your grid. You will be amazed at what a beautiful life begins to emerge—so rich, full, loving, and giving. It is important to keep in mind that whatever you create in your grid can become a reality—if you are committed to taking the necessary action.

7. Each day, create for yourself specific goals that reflect all the boxes in your grid. If you are already a diligent daily goal setter, you will probably notice that your goals are focused in only one area of your life—most likely work. By setting goals for all areas of your grid, your life will become balanced.

As you approach each goal, bear in mind the Magic Duo—*100% commitment* and *I count*—to help you focus and achieve a sense of fulfillment.

You may not be able to cover every area of your grid every day. Naturally, there will be times in your life when one area takes precedence. For example, when on vacation you can forget about other areas of the grid. Just concentrate on having a good time. The Magic Duo will ensure that you take it all in. In the same manner, an important work project may require your undivided attention for a time. What you are ultimately looking for is overall balance.

APPLYING THE GRID TO YOUR LIFE

1. Recognize that you might be caught in a vicious circle when you've suffered a loss.

2. Create your own Whole Life Grid and fill it in.

3. Pick one of your boxes and visualize how you want that part of your life to look.

4. Write down your visualization.

5. Make a list of what you can do to achieve your mental picture.

6. Repeat Steps 3, 4, and 5 for each area of your grid.

7. Create specific goals every day that reflect all the boxes on your grid.

Consider this: If you don't feel like taking the time or making the effort to do these steps, you will be greatly shortchanging yourself. Isn't your life worth it? What I'm asking you to do is to set up the basic structure of your life, so you can then go on living in a way that supports your growth and satisfaction. As Gita, one of my students, so aptly put it, "If you always do what you've always done, you'll always get what you've always got." This thought certainly served to get her moving!

If you find it difficult to motivate yourself, don't put yourself down. Find a self-help group to act as a catalyst. If you can't find a support group, find what I call a "growth buddy." You and your buddy can help each other by meeting weekly and working on the grid, your goals, your action plan, or whatever. Committing yourself to do certain homework before each meeting often spurs you on to action. The key is to take your commitment to your buddy seriously and act responsibly during the week by getting everything done that you committed yourself to do.

If you can't find a self-help group and do not want to work with a growth buddy, find a group conducted by a social worker, life coach, or other care professional. There are so many alternatives these days. It is amazing how quickly results materialize when you know what you want and are determined to get it. Most people never take the time to focus on what they want—then they wonder why they always feel empty.

Keep asking yourself, "How whole is my life?" Continue to create such abundance for yourself that nothing can ever take away your basic sense of completeness. Can you imagine how little you would then have to fear?

9.

Just Nod Your Head— Say Yes!

One of the most valuable lessons in learning to diminish fear is embodied in the phrase SAY YES TO YOUR UNIVERSE. These words were casually uttered by Janet Zuckerman, a wonderful teacher of mine, to someone who was complaining bitterly about a particular circumstance in his life. I asked Janet exactly what she meant by that phrase, and she replied, "It's simple. Whatever happens to you in life, just nod your head, up and down, instead of shaking it, side to side. Just say yes instead of no." Over the years I've incorporated this phrase into my life with magical results.

The term "universe" refers to that life plan that seems to take over despite what we have in mind—that "force" operating, seemingly on its own, that often interferes with our picture of how we would like things to be. It refers to a certain flow in our lives and the lives of others over which we have little or no control. So often when we are all set to move in a specific direction, an unexpected event changes everything. Those unexpected events or even the possibility of the unexpected sets us up for a great deal of fear.

We often fear the worst, even when good stuff is happening to us. The mindfulness and vulnerability author Brené Brown named this feeling "Foreboding Joy" in her book *Daring Greatly*. When we are confronted with change and the unknown, even things that could be joy-filled, many of us spoil our happiness by waiting for something bad to happen. She says, "When we lose the ability or willingness to be vulnerable, joy becomes something we approach with deep foreboding." In these circumstances, saying yes becomes an act of vulnerability; it means letting go of fear and trusting—ourselves and the universe.

When we anticipate the worst, it is important to remember:

• • •

In saying yes lies the antidote to our fear.

• • •

The phrase "say yes" means "to agree to" those things that life hands us. Saying yes means letting go of resistance and letting in the possibilities that our universe offers in new ways of seeing the world. It means to relax bodily, to calmly survey the situation, thereby reducing upset and anxiety. Aside from the emotional benefits, the physical benefits are enormous. Saying *yes* allows us to be the creators of our lives, rather than victims of circumstance. *Yes* makes us feel connected and allows us to move forward in a way that helps heal our own lives and the world around us.

Conversely, saying no means to be a victim. "How could this happen to me!" Saying no means to block, to fight, to resist opportunities for growth and challenge. Saying no creates tension, exhaustion, wasted expenditure of energy, emotional upheaval—or worse, it creates apathy. "I can't cope. I can't go on. There is no hope." The truth of the matter is that saying yes is our only hope.

Not only is saying yes our antidote to dealing with day-to-day disappointments, rejections, and missed opportunities (the flu, a leaking roof, a traffic jam, a flat tire, a lousy date, and so on), *it is the miracle tool for dealing with our deepest, darkest fears.*

Charles

Let me tell you about Charles, whose presence in my life confirmed the power of saying yes to the universe. Charles grew up in poverty in New York. His "tough guy" image served him well until he was severely handicapped by a gunshot wound incurred in a street fight. His spine was shattered, and he was paralyzed from the waist down.

When I met Charles, he had just completed training in a rehabilitation center and was looking for a job at the Floating Hospital. Charles wanted an opportunity to teach children how to avoid getting into trouble the way he had. He became part of my staff and an inspiration to everyone around him.

One day I walked into one of our classrooms and found Charles sitting with a group of children surrounding him. He was answering all the burning questions that young people have when they look at a person in a wheelchair. "What does it feel like not to be able to walk?" "What should I say to someone in a wheelchair?" "How do you go to the bathroom?" At one point, Charles asked the group what they thought a person with disabilities wanted most. One little boy quickly answered, "Friends!" "Right!" answered Charles, and all the children spontaneously jumped up and hugged him, shouting, "I'll be your friend!" I don't know who got more out of the session—Charles, the children, or me.

On another occasion, we were giving a party for a new group of senior citizens. Although we had hired a three-piece band for the festivities, the seniors were hesitant about getting into the swing of things. All of a sudden, Charles pushed his wheelchair into the middle of the room and started dancing with the music. "Come on, everyone. If I can get out here and dance, so can you." Within minutes, he had everyone dancing, laughing, singing, and clapping. His spirit was infectious. The strangers in the room quickly became friends. He never missed the opportunity to show people that, with a positive attitude, value can be created from anything that happens to you in life.

I had many opportunities to talk with Charles. He told me that in the early days of his disability he had lost all hope, all will. As he described it, "It wasn't easy for a macho kid to lose his ability to walk, let alone to lose all control of his bladder and bowels." He was referred to an excellent rehabilitation center, but refused to be helped. The center was about to send him home to make way for someone who was willing to take responsibility for his own life. That was the turning point. Charles knew that if he was sent home, he would have no chance at all. This was his moment to say *yes* or *no* to his universe. He is thankful he chose to say *yes*.

Once that choice was made, his progress was remarkable. Opportunities opened up to him that he'd never thought about before. He decided that his life could have a purpose: to help others in their struggle, whatever that struggle might be. He would be a model, saying, "If I could do it, so can you." Charles admitted to me that, strangely, he was grateful now for his disabilities, because they made him aware of how much he had to contribute to the world.

Before the accident, Charles had been blind to the fact that his life had meaning. Now he believes he was more limited before the accident; only since then has he derived satisfaction from living.

When I presented the concept of SAY YES TO YOUR UNIVERSE in class, one of my students asked an interesting question: "If you always say *yes* to your universe, wouldn't you be able to avoid feeling any pain?" I thought about it for a moment and told him no. You can't avoid pain, but you can say *yes* to the pain, understanding that it is a part of life. You do not, then, feel yourself a victim. You know that you can handle the pain, as well as the situation causing the pain. You do not feel it is hopeless. At that point, my student shouted, "I get it! You mean there is the pain of *yes* versus the pain of *no*." That was exactly what I meant.

As the class looked at it further, they were able to find examples of when they had said *yes* to pain in their lives without realizing what they were doing. Eric remembered one day the previous week when he thought about his mother, who had recently died. Suddenly he was struck by the pain of loss. He sat down and cried, thinking how strangely sweet it felt to remember back to good times he had shared with his mother. And as he cried, he felt the urge to say "thanks" over and over again.

He was aware, in the middle of his pain, that life hands you a lot of goodbyes—but that's just the way life is. Yet he saw the difference between handling the death of a loved one as a catastrophe (saying *no*) and keeping in mind how blessed he was to have had that person in his life (saying *yes*). It is seeing death as part of living—a natural process—as opposed to seeing it as a horrible deprivation and unjust phenomenon.

Latrice, another student, remembered the sweetness of the pain she felt as she kissed her son goodbye when she moved him into his dorm room at college. She had tears in her eyes as she and her husband drove home without him. It was now time to let him go. She reported thinking, *yes*, this is the way life is . . . always changing. Things don't last forever. She let herself reminisce for a while, but soon picked herself up. She planned a romantic dinner for her and her husband the following weekend. After all, she and her husband would be alone for the first time in many years, so she was determined to make a honeymoon of it.

Compare this with a parent who dreads their children leaving home, and when it finally happens is able to see only the emptiness of the house and the uselessness of their life. Such a person, resisting change, misses the new pathways opening up for them. Latrice's story beautifully demonstrates the ability to feel pain when something ends but then to go on and build new hopes and dreams for oneself. There is something enriching about leaving one beautiful experience in your life and looking forward to other beautiful experiences.

Margo shared with the class the pain she felt when her husband died. Yes, she missed her husband and the warmth and companionship he had given her, but she was also aware of how she had transformed herself from a dependent to an independent person when left to her own resources. Her sense of self-esteem had increased enormously as she slowly learned to take risks she had never taken before. She was able to say *yes* to life and create a whole new world for herself.

Margo could have reacted like a friend of mine did. Nick refused to pick up the pieces and go on after his wife died. Five years later, he is still crying on the phone, asking, "Why did she have to die?" He has said *no* to his universe. Unfortunately, Nick doesn't see that the universe isn't suffering, only he is, and perhaps the few people who still talk to him on the phone. He has refused to see the blessings in his life—and there are many—or the opportunities around him to meet new people and try new experiences. The pain of *no* leaves him feeling powerless.

Another student, Noah, was struggling with having to move back in with his parents after his relationship ended. He was 35 and had a good job as a carpenter, but he couldn't afford to get his own apartment. With his current salary, he knew it would be a long time before he could afford to rent or buy his own place.

He felt ashamed of his situation and, as a result, he pulled away from his circle of friends. "Saying Yes" was a hard lesson for Noah to learn. He was fixated on what his life "should" be rather than acknowledging what his current circumstances were. Instead of making plans to move forward from where he was, he lamented all that he had lost. It took him a while to see that while the door on his old life had closed there were plenty of open doors ahead of him to choose from.

In the final analysis, it can be said that your ability to cope effectively with the world around you corresponds to your ability to say *yes* to your universe, including the pain. Remember:

• • •

Acknowledgment of pain is very important; denial is deadly.

• • •

Sophia is someone who avoided her pain. When her son died in an automobile accident 12 years ago, she never faced the full impact of the loss. Friends remarked on how well she had handled her son's death. Three years later, she developed epilepsy, which seemed to be unrelated to the loss she had experienced. For nine years she suffered from seizures that prevented her from working. In addition, her relationships with her husband and other children were slowly deteriorating.

Sophia finally went to a support group to get help in dealing with the upset the epilepsy was creating within the family. During the first session, the group leader, a psychologist, asked if she had ever suffered a great loss. She said yes, but explained that it had happened so long ago it was no longer a factor in her life. He knew better and with great skill managed to get her back into the experience of her son's death. He explained that new studies suggest that a person can develop post-traumatic stress disorder (PTSD) after the unexpected death of a loved one. It was then that she finally allowed her grief to emerge.

Each time the group met, Sophia continued to deal with her

pain. Astonishingly, her epileptic symptoms disappeared within a few months. She discontinued her medication, found a good job, and began to repair the damage done within her home as a result of her PTSD. Pain can be incredibly destructive if kept submerged. Although Sophia's story is a dramatic example, unacknowledged pain and the health conditions it can cause are subtly destroying many people's lives.

We all know people who are out of touch with their pain—who have refused to let themselves feel their emotions. When we don't acknowledge our pain, it will be transferred into a bodily symptom, a condition or illness, anger, depression or despair, or something equally destructive. Saying *yes* means letting in the pain full force, knowing you will not only get to the other side of it, but also gain something in the end—if you look for it.

As the class discussions continued, my students and I came up with an interesting thought: the richer our lives, the more likely we are to experience the pain of loss. If we have a multitude of friends, we will have to deal with more goodbyes. The more we are able to reach out into the world, the greater the likelihood that we are going to experience "failure" or rejection. But those who are living rich lives wouldn't change them for a moment. They delight in the opportunity to taste all that life has to offer—the good and the bad. The class also decided that it is likely that those who lead rich lives intuitively know the secret of saying yes to the universe. Those who say no usually withdraw from life, choosing symbolically to hide under the covers to keep themselves from becoming victims—ironically, ending up complete victims of their own fears.

I found the most extreme and moving example of saying yes in the pages of Viktor Frankl's book *Man's Search for Meaning*. It was given to me by a friend, who said, "I think it's really important for you to read this book."

I was upset to learn that the book was about Frankl's experience in a concentration camp—a subject I had carefully avoided. It was simply too frightening for me to look at. I had viewed life in a concentration camp as the most terrible experience a human being could endure—mentally, physically, and spiritually. I really didn't want to read this book and was about to put it aside when my friend's words came back to me: "I think it's really important for you to read this book." She obviously knew something I didn't, so I decided to find out what she was talking about.

I painfully pushed through page after page of description that defied human comprehension. I couldn't keep back my tears. But as I continued to read, my heart slowly started to lighten. Not only had Frankl and others like him faced life in a concentration camp, but, according to the definition given earlier, *they had actually said yes to their universe!* They were able to create a positive experience out of what life had handed them. They were able to find personal meaning and growth—and a way of seeing the world that created value from their experience. As Frankl wrote:

> *The experiences of camp life show that a man does have a choice of action. There were enough examples, often of a heroic nature, which proved that apathy could be overcome, irritability suppressed. Man can preserve a vestige of spiritual freedom, of independence of mind, even in such terrible conditions of psychic and physical stress. We who lived in concentration camps can remember the men who walked through the huts comforting others, giving away their last piece of bread. They may have been few in number, but they offer sufficient proof that everything can be taken away from a man but one thing: the last of the human freedoms—to choose one's attitude in any given set of circumstances, to choose one's way. The way in which a man accepts his fate and all the suffering it entails, the way in which he takes up his cross, gives him ample opportunity—even in the most difficult circumstances—to add a deeper meaning to his life.*

As I finished the last page, I knew that a dramatic change had taken place within me. I would never again experience fear with the same intensity I had experienced it before reading the book. I knew that if Frankl was able to create something positive out of his experience, which was the worst my mind could imagine, then I—and everyone else—could create value out of anything life could possibly hand us. It is a matter of remaining conscious that we have the choice.

I am sure that, given the option, Frankl would have preferred not to go through the experience, but the concentration camp was what life handed him. It was then up to him to create his reaction to the situation. We can't control the world, but we can control our reactions to it. I think you now begin to see how SAY YES TO YOUR UNIVERSE can work, not only to reduce fear, but also to create meaning in life.

During another class, one of my students argued that if we say *yes* to everything, we are accepting everything. If we accept everything, then we won't act to change things that are wrong with this world. I explained to him that saying *yes* means positive action; saying *no* means giving up. It is only when we see *possibility* for change that we can work to effect change. We can say *no* to the situation as it is, but *yes* to the possibility for the growth it offers. If you believe a situation in your life is hopeless, you simply sit back and let yourself be destroyed.

On a global level, if you believe it is hopeless to halt nuclear war, you won't get involved in standing up for peaceful solutions to the world's problems. If you know this situation is not hopeless, you say yes to the opportunity to get involved in the process of making ours a peaceful planet, as so many people are doing throughout the world. These people are not paralyzed by fear, because they are saying *yes* to the opportunities inherent in the situation.

Saying *yes* does not mean giving up.

• • •

Saying yes means getting up and acting on your belief that you can create meaning and purpose in whatever life hands you.

• • •

It means channeling resources to find constructive, healthy ways to deal with adverse situations. It means acting out of strength, not weakness. It means having the flexibility necessary to survey many options and choose ones that enhance growth. It does not mean being destroyed; it means becoming alive to possibility.

Whereas the concept of saying *yes* to your universe is fairly easy to grasp, learning to say *yes* requires a great deal of awareness. We seem to have an automatic reflex that pushes the *no* button. We often automatically feel that negative thinking is more realistic than positive thinking. It is not so easy to understand how to say *yes* when a child is gravely ill, when you become physically disabled, when you lose your job, or when a loved one dies. Remember:

. . .

The world is filled with people who have been handed the "worst" life has to offer . . . and they have come out winners!

. . .

We are all winners when we say *yes*, and it is worth every effort to learn how. The following steps will help:

1. Create *awareness* that you are saying *no*. It helps to surround yourself with reminders. Put signs on your desk, on your night table, on your mirrors, in your daily calendar, or wherever you'll see them. Some signs that helped me were SAY YES TO YOUR UNIVERSE (an obvious one); I AM FINDING VALUE IN EVERYTHING THAT HAPPENS TO ME; YOU ARE NEVER TOO OLD TO SET ANOTHER GOAL OR DREAM ANOTHER DREAM; and THE DIFFERENCE BETWEEN WINNING AND LOSING IS, MOST OFTEN, NOT QUITTING. My daughter gave me a wonderful poster with the oldie-but-goodie expression IF LIFE GIVES YOU LEMONS, MAKE LEMONADE.

You can create your own sayings that work best for you. The object is to stay *conscious*. We are asleep on this issue and need constantly to be reminded.

2. Once consciousness is there, *actually nod your head up and down; say yes*. There is something about physically affirming an idea that helps to create acceptance. Try nodding your head right now. You'll notice you feel something positive about the feeling of physically nodding in agreement. It gives you the sense that everything will be all right—because you are going to make it all right.

3. Using the same principle, physically relax your body, starting from the top of your head and going to the tip of your toes. Notice where you are tense, and focus on letting the tension go. Again, the body can take the lead in setting up positive feelings. This is discussed later.

4. Look for ways to create value from any experience. Ask yourself these questions: What can I learn from the experience? How can I use this experience to positive advantage? How can I learn to better myself as a result of this experience? Simply having the intent to create something positive automatically ensures that something positive will happen. As discussed in Chapter 7, let go of the picture of what the outcome "should" be, to open the way for possibilities your mind is incapable of envisioning.

5. Be patient with yourself: DON'T SAY *NO* TO YOUR DIFFICULTY IN SAYING *YES*. This is one of those concepts that seems easy but requires diligence to put into practice. It is easy to feel frustrated when gloom and doom overtake you. Just keep noticing this. Trust that you'll eventually get bored being depressed or upset, and you'll then find a way out of the quicksand. Most of us do anyway. Saying *yes* helps you find your way much faster, thus vastly improving the quality of your life.

One additional tip may be helpful. Start practicing on trivial events in your life. Although they may have nothing to do with fear, they will give you practice with the process. For example, as you sit in your car, fuming because of a traffic jam, a sign on the dashboard that reads SAY YES TO YOUR UNIVERSE may remind you that you are saying *no*. Once you can create this awareness, you can nod your head, relax your body, and begin to use the experience to some advantage. You can use such time to listen to music, a great inspirational audio, the audio version of that book you wanted to read but could never find the time for, or a humorous podcast. Or you can be grateful that while stuck in traffic for the moment, nothing very taxing is demanded of you. So sit back and enjoy the experience.

If you are worried that you are keeping someone waiting, remember that there is nothing you can do about it, so you might as well relax. It is a perfect opportunity to learn that in the future you will need to allow more time for unexpected delays.

If you are on the other end, waiting, muttering to yourself, "They're late again!" focus on saying yes to the fact that you now have an opportunity to people-watch or reflect on the day's activities. I'm one of those people who loves to wait. It gives me a rare opportunity to do nothing without feeling guilty!

Life offers many opportunities to practice saying yes to your universe. Your pet had an accident on the floor; you didn't save the letter you were writing and your computer crashed; your mobile phone battery died when you really needed to send a text; the cleaner ruined your shirt—get the picture? Every time you find yourself resisting what's happening at the present moment, recall the phrase SAY YES TO YOUR UNIVERSE. You will watch your life become more and more pleasurable. Relationships with the whole world will improve dramatically.

Once you master the concept on a day-to-day level, you will be prepared to handle the more serious issues that confront you. You will notice your level of fear slowly starts to drop as it is replaced by a greater sense of trust in your ability to handle your world. As you start to see the possibilities in the impossible, you will begin to see that the world works "perfectly." You can find reason and purpose in everything—if you open your mind to it.

In *End the Struggle and Dance with Life*, I wrote about an idea first put forth by the inspirational author Alan Cohen—

"What if this were alright?" When you're faced with a frustrating, sad, annoying, or angry moment, what would it be like if it were alright? That's definitely a different way of thinking for most of us, me included!

Try this exercise to really incorporate the idea into your SAY YES TO THE UNIVERSE thinking.

· · ·

What if this were alright?

· · ·

Begin by writing down all of the situations in your life that are causing you upset. Then ask yourself the same question about each one . . . "What if this were alright?" Each time you ask this question, take a deep breath and relax. You will experience a momentary feeling of peace. Do this over and over again until just the asking of the question is associated with a deep breath and a feeling of relaxation. And as you go through each day, notice where you are resisting experiences. Add it to your list and keep asking yourself the question "What if this were all alright?"

The only time you will fear anything is when you say no and resist the universe. You may have heard the expression "Go with the flow." This means consciously accepting what is happening in your life. I once heard it said that the key to life is not to figure out what you can get from the flow, but rather to figure out how to get into the flow. Or, as the therapist and writer Barry Stevens titled her book, *Don't Push the River* (it flows by itself). Stop fighting your life. Let go and let the river carry you to new adventures by the way you experience your life. In this way—and only in this way—it is impossible to lose.

STEPS TO SAYING YES

1. Create awareness that you can choose to say *yes* or *no*.

2. Nod your head—say *yes*.

3. Relax your body.

4. Adopt an attitude of "It's all happening perfectly. Let's see what good I can create from this situation."

5. Be patient with yourself. It takes times to adopt a *yes* approach to life. Say *yes* to you!

hing to fear I am powerful and I am loving and I have nothing to fear I am powerful and I am
I have nothing to fear I am powerful and I am loving and I have nothing to fear I am power
n loving and I have nothing to fear I am powerful and I am loving and I have nothing to fear
werful and I am loving and I have nothing to fear I am powerful and I am loving and I have n
r I am powerful and I am loving and I have nothing to fear I am powerful and I am loving and
hing to fear I am powerful and I am loving and I have nothing to fear I am powerful and I am
I have nothing to fear I am powerful and I am loving and I have nothing to fear I am power
n loving and I have nothing to fear I am powerful and I am loving and I have nothing to fear
werful and I am loving and I have nothing to fear I am powerful and I am loving and I have n
r I am powerful and I am loving and I have nothing to fear I am powerful and I am loving and
hing to fear I am powerful and I am loving and I have nothing to fear I am powerful and I am

I have nothing to fe   g to fear I am power
n loving and I have nc   have nothing to fear
werful and I am loving   n loving and I have ne
r I am powerful and I   I and I am loving and
hing to fear I am pow   m powerful and I am
I have nothing to fe   g to fear I am power

10.

Choosing Love and Trust

n loving and I have nc   have nothing to fear
werful and I am loving   n loving and I have nc
r I am powerful and I   I and I am loving and
hing to fear I am pow   m powerful and I am
I have nothing to fe   g to fear I am powert
n loving and I have nc   have nothing to fear
werful and I am loving   n loving and I have nc
r I am powerful and I   I and I am loving and
hing to fear I am pow   m powerful and I am
I have nothing to fe   g to fear I am powerf
n loving and I have nc   have nothing to fear I

werful and I am loving and I have nothing to fear I am powerful and I am loving and I have nc
r I am powerful and I am loving and I have nothing to fear I am powerful and I am loving and
hing to fear I am powerful and I am loving and I have nothing to fear I am powerful and I am
I have nothing to fear I am powerful and I am loving and I have nothing to fear I am powerf
n loving and I have nothing to fear I am powerful and I am loving and I have nothing to fear I
werful and I am loving and I have nothing to fear I am powerful and I am loving and I have nc
I am powerful and I am loving and I have nothing to fear I am powerful and I am loving and
hing to fear I am powerful and I am loving and I have nothing to fear I am powerful and I am
I have nothing to fear I am powerful and I am loving and I have nothing to fear I am powerf
a loving and I have nothing to fear I am powerful and I am loving and I have nothing to fear I
werful and I am loving and I have nothing to fear I am powerful and I am loving and I have nc
I am powerful and I am loving and I have nothing to fear I am powerful and I am loving and
hing to fear I am powerful and I am loving and I have nothing to fear I am powerful and I am
I have nothing to fear I am powerful and I am loving and I have nothing to fear I am powerf
n loving and I have nothing to fear I am powerful and I am loving and I have nothing to fear I
werful and I am loving and I have nothing to fear I am powerful and I am loving and I have nc
I am powerful and I am loving and I have nothing to fear I am powerful and I am loving and

Do you consider yourself a giving person? Think about it for a moment.

I asked this question of some of my students one morning, most of whom were in a committed relationship, and they all nodded, meaning yes. Therefore, they were bewildered by their own reactions to the homework assignment I then gave them, which was simply, "Go home and say 'thank you' to your significant other." There was a distinct sense of discomfort in the room. You would have thought I had asked them to go home and beat their pets! Finally, Lottie, who had been married for 25 years, piped up with "Why should I say thank you to my husband? He should be glad I'm there!"

"Lottie, why *are* you there?" I asked. Her response was rather evasive—something to the effect that "he'd be a mess without me, and, besides, it would be too much trouble to leave." I repeated my question. After much prodding from me and the rest of the class, Lottie finally was able to acknowledge that her husband gave her a number of advantages: companionship, financial security, and the feeling that she was not alone. I said, "Fine, so go home and thank him for that."

The following session brought the students into class wearing looks of dismay. They couldn't believe how difficult it had been to acknowledge the contribution of a partner. Some were able to do the assignment, though with reluctance; others simply could not do it at all. Some reported that they also tried to thank their children and parents, and that, too, was very difficult. For the first time, they were forced to question just how giving they really were.

This did not mean that they were not contributing in other areas of their relationships. For the most part, they handled the details of sharing a home—supporting it financially, engaging with their partner. But were they really giving? Did they really know how to give? Or did they just exchange a "you do this for me" with an "I'll do this for you."

Needless to say, my students were quite dismayed by what they had discovered about themselves in this simple assignment. I assured them that most of us in our society do not really know how to give. Most of us operate on a hidden barter system. Few genuinely ever give anything away without expecting something in return—money, appreciation, love, or whatever.

You might be saying, "What's wrong with getting back?" My answer is "Nothing." However:

. . .

If all your "giving" is about "getting," think how fearful you will become.

. . .

More than likely the question will soon become "Am I getting back *enough*?" This kind of thinking sets up an incredible need to control others so you won't feel shortchanged; it destroys your peace of mind and creates anger and resentment.

Now you can see what's wrong with "getting" being the most important motivation for "giving." In fact:

. . .

Genuine giving is not only altruistic; it also makes us feel better.

. . .

Why do we find it so difficult to give? My theory has two components. First, it requires a mature adult to give, and most of us have never really grown up. I consider an adult to be someone who takes responsibility for their own experience of life. Someone who is secure in themself, who doesn't blame, and who expects to contribute their fair share. An adult is someone who keeps their word, appreciates what they have, and doesn't take things for granted. Can you see why most of us have never really grown up? Second, giving is an acquired skill that few of us have mastered. These components are tied together and require a great deal of practice to achieve.

The reason most of us have never practiced these skills is simple—it usually never occurs to us that we aren't behaving like adults or that we aren't giving. We unwittingly have deceived ourselves. This is understandable. We *look* like we are adults and we *seem* to be giving people. What's going on underneath, however, belies appearances.

One of the most important lessons to learn in life is how to give, and *therein lies an answer to fear*. As babies we represent the ultimate of neediness. We come into this world as total takers. We have to take, or we will die. Our survival is tied up with the world nurturing us. We give little back. We don't care what time we wake our parents when we are hungry, or how loudly we scream and bother the neighbors when we want to be picked up.

Yes, parents often get a feeling of joy from the smile or the touch of their child and, in that sense, the child is a giver—but I doubt if the child spent the night pondering: "My life is abundant. I have so much to give away that I think I'll reward my parents with a great big smile tomorrow morning." No, their "gift" is on a rather primitive or reflexive level. In fact, a hungry belly in the morning will produce only loud shrieks of impatience.

As the years pass, we function as more and more independent beings, able to take care of ourselves—or so it appears. We dress ourselves, we feed ourselves, we earn a living. Yet there seems to be a part of us that never progresses much beyond the crib. Metaphorically, we remain frightened that no one will come to relieve our hunger—for food, money, love, praise, and so on. Any relief in the way of "food" is only temporary; we know the hunger will come again.

Imagine what this dilemma sets up for us in the area of our daily living. We can't give. We can't love. We become, consciously or unconsciously, manipulative, because our survival is involved. We can't support the well-being of another person if their needs in any way conflict with ours. And how do we feel operating from the level of the playpen? Helpless, trapped, angry, frustrated, dissatisfied, unfulfilled, and, most of all, *fearful*.

What can be more frightening than depending on someone else for one's survival? As fearful adults, we ask the same questions we did as a child. Will they go away and not come back? Will they stop loving me? Will they take care of me? Will they get sick and die? As adults, we ask these questions about our mates, and often about our friends, bosses, parents, and even our children.

People who fear can't genuinely give. They are imbued with a deep-seated sense of scarcity in the world, as if there wasn't enough to go around. Not enough love, not enough money, not enough praise, not enough attention—simply not enough. Usually fear in one area of our lives generalizes, and we become closed down and protective in many areas of our lives. Fearful people can be visualized as crouched and hugging themselves. Whereas this image represents the inner state of all frightened people, the outer manifestation can take on many forms:

Successful professionals needing the boss's approval
Stay-at-home parents who blame their partners or
     children for the fact that they never lived their own
     lives
Independent people who prioritize their career, don't
     make time for a relationship, and find themselves alone
People who can't tolerate their partner's independence
Company executives who make harmful, irresponsible
     decisions
Grown children who blame their parents for problems of
     their own making
Friends who demand attention and compliments
People who dabble in relationships but are fearful of
     commitment

They are all in some way operating out of a sense of fear for their own survival. They are reacting to their lack of trust. They all are, in effect, crouched and withholding inside.

If you recognize yourself in this description, join the rest of us. There are few in our society who have actually been taught the secrets of growing up and giving. We have been taught the illusion of giving, but not the actuality of giving. As we have been taught to be careful in terms of our physical safety, we have also been taught not to let anyone take advantage of us. As a result, unless we get something back, we feel used.

This is not to say that we can't enjoy what comes back to us, and paradoxically:

· · ·

When we give from a place of love, rather than from a place of expectation, more usually comes back to us than we could ever have imagined.

· · ·

But if we are constantly expecting, we will spend a great deal of our lives disappointed that the world isn't treating us right.

I didn't find my way out of this painful state of existence until my mid-30s, when it finally dawned on me that no matter how much I had in my life, *nothing would ever be enough!* The more I had, the more I wanted—more love, more money, more praise—more, more, more. Obviously, something I was or wasn't doing was keeping me from ever feeling satisfied. And, worse, it was keeping me in a state of constant fear that everything I had would ultimately disappear and there would be nothing left. I saw everything as the proverbial last drink of water in the desert, and I hung on for dear life.

It was time to try another way of being, since my old way was definitely not serving me, or anyone else in my life. As I described earlier, I sought out many teachers and got many answers. In essence, I learned that in order to get rid of the fear of lack, I had to do the *opposite* of what I had been doing up until that time. Instead of hanging on to everything for dear life, I had to start releasing, letting go, giving it away. If you think anything else in this book is difficult, wait until you try this one! It's really a catch-22: it's easy to give *when* you feel abundantly endowed, but you only feel that way when you give, not before! So: FEEL THE FEAR . . . AND DO IT ANYWAY!

Again let me remind you that what I am presenting is a life-long process that you can begin working on today. There is no magical potion as yet. It is amazing how long it takes to become a full-blown adult. In fact, one might consider it a lifelong task. I've been working on this for years and I'm still working on it. The good news, however, is that my sense of personal power and my ability to love and trust have increased at least 1,000% since I have been practicing giving it away. Many fears in the areas discussed below have completely disappeared for me. The rewards are monumental. I promise!

THE TOOLS FOR LIVING A GIVING LIFE
Give Away Thanks

Start by thinking about the people presently in your life and significant ones in your past. Put their names on a sheet of paper. Then list what each of them contributed to you in their own special way. Even if they brought you pain and you dislike them intensely, list their contribution to your life. As with Lottie, earlier, despite what she felt about her husband, there was much that he had provided for her. Also, it's possible to make a gift even out of a negative.

I apologized to my son one day for the fact that at the time I got divorced I wasn't there for him emotionally when he might have needed me. I was too wrapped up in my own pain to help him with his. His answer was "It's okay, Mom. That was the period of my life when I learned independence. That was a valuable lesson." He was able to thank me for my lack! In terms of mental health, he was far better off than if he had carried around resentment all those years. So, even if you perceive that someone has mistreated you, find the lesson you learned from them and put the contribution on your list.

Once you have listed all the gifts from various people in your life, systematically go about thanking them. If it is someone you haven't seen or heard from in a while, surprise them with a call or an email simply acknowledging what they have contributed to your life. You will be amazed at the pleasure you will get—and give—from doing this.

With some people in your life, such as an ex-partner, former friends or bosses, alienated parents or children, this can be especially difficult. To help rid yourself of present feelings of resentment and anger, try this visualization I learned in a workshop many moons ago:

Visualizing Gratitude

Find an empty room and turn off any electronics that might interrupt you. Put on some soothing music. Sit down in a comfortable chair and close your eyes. Visualize someone who brings up a lot of anger or pain in you. Picture them in front of you. First, surround them with rays of healing white light and tell them that you wish them all good things—everything they could possibly want in their lifetime. Thank them for whatever they have given you. Keep doing this until you feel your negative emotions leaving.

To say this is not easy is to utter the biggest understatement in the world. "Wish *her* good things? Are you out of your mind? I want to see her suffer for what she's done to me!"

The first time I did this exercise, I picked someone who had previously worked for me and who had caused me a great deal of upset and pain. I had trusted him, and, to my mind, he had betrayed me. Note the victim mentality in full bloom! Obviously I was not taking responsibility for my experience of life at that time. As I went through the exercise, I experienced an incredible series of emotions.

First, I was shocked at the anger and resentment I was holding. I found it almost impossible, even in my mind's eye, to wish him anything good. My initial anger toward him was monumental. As I slowly released the anger, I got in touch with the pain I felt. This turned to anger at myself for allowing what had happened and for holding all my anger for so long. This turned into forgiveness of myself and of him. I was able to see both of us simply as people who had done the best we could at the time. I could then surround us both with healing white light.

This process took about an hour. When I began, I thought nothing much would happen. Wrong! I screamed, I cried, I hurt, I hated, I opened up, I forgave, I loved, I felt peace. I continued to do this exercise daily until I no longer felt anything negative about him and could freely wish him all good things.

I did this exercise for all the people in my life for whom I was holding any negativity, no matter how great or how slight. One of the people was my ex-husband. When I was able to reach the point in my visualization when I wished him only good, I phoned him and invited him to lunch. I simply said that there were some things I'd never told him and I wanted to do so now. He was pleased I called and we met for lunch.

I told him all the things that I really did appreciate about him when we were married and the qualities in him that I admire. My openness invited openness on his part, and he shared things about me that were loving as well. When I left lunch that day, I felt I had completed something that heretofore had been incomplete—and it felt wonderful.

If you cannot actually meet with people on your list, do it in your mind. Talk to them as if they were sitting in front of you and tell them what you want to say. Heal the relationship within yourself. In terms of your physical and mental health, it is just as good as if they were actually sitting before you.

We need to get rid of pain and anger before we can bring in love. When we hold negative feelings about people in our past, we carry those feelings to those in our present. Not only that, but we can make ourselves physically ill, as some of you may have already experienced. An excellent book to read on the subject of healing your body and mind is Louise Hay's *You Can Heal Your Life*. She has many exercises that will help you release the anger, pain, and resentment that you may be carrying around with you.

So many people don't say thank you because they don't realize how important their thanks may be. It could make a huge difference to someone, the difference between a good day and a bad day. We all want to be acknowledged positively. Thanking someone—friends, strangers, lovers, family—lets them know that you see them. Remember, *you count and your thanks count*. Don't let an opportunity go by to thank someone who has given you something—anything at all.

If this seems difficult for you right now, start with casual situations, such as saying to someone at work: "Thank you for that" or "I appreciate that" or "Thank you for being happy today; it's made me happy." *Thank you, thank you, thank you*. Start getting those words into your consciousness about everyone around you. Start thanking others instead of waiting for thanks to come to you. It is tough in the beginning, but it gets easier. Giving away thanks is like a muscle to be used. As we flex it, it gets stronger. It just takes exercise.

Give Away Attention

This can also be described as giving away notice and is closely associated with giving away thanks and praise. With so many of us spending our days with our nose pointed at a screen of some sort, attention to other people feels like it is fading away. Just recently, I was driving my car, listening to a fascinating audiobook, and just about to turn into a parking lot when out of nowhere a young man walked in front of my car, his eyes firmly planted on his mobile phone screen. Had I not been intending to turn, I would have been hard-pressed not to run him over. While I sat at the wheel in shock from the close call, the young man never even noticed!

While this is an extreme example, I'm sure there are times when you are so caught up in your own thinking (or internet browsing) that you don't notice the goings-on around you.

Small children often demand the attention of their parents or other adults. They need that attention to validate the new things they learn, the new ideas they have, even their individual identity. Just because we grow out of demanding attention doesn't mean we don't still need it. Humans are social animals and it's important for us to be acknowledged by our fellow humans. When you are going through the checkout line in a grocery store, do you take the time to notice the person checking you out? Do you look them in the eyes to respond to their question: "Did you find everything okay?" Or do you mumble your reply while looking for your wallet? When you enter a store, do your eyes go right to the cases and racks of items for sale instead of the person who greets you as you walk through the door? You get the picture.

Attention is one of the easiest and meaningful things we can give away. Pay attention to giving away attention.

Give Away Information

So much of what we learn in life comes to us with great difficulty. And, for some reason, we have a tendency to want to see others struggle as much as we did. Turn this around and begin giving others as much help as you can possibly give them. Professionally, this can be very difficult. I can remember times when I felt threatened by those I felt were my "competition," and the tendency was to withhold information from them that would help them in their work.

Thank goodness, I felt the fear . . . and did it anyway. Some of the people I helped have become my good friends and part of my support system. Especially here, the giving has to be done with no expectations of return. More likely than not, however, the return will be enormous. One of my students asked what would have happened if one of them really had turned against me and used my information in a competitive way. My answer was, and is, that if I have enough belief in myself that I will "make it" no matter what anyone does, what is there to fear? It's a matter of developing trust in yourself and in your universe. For some reason, when you become a support to others you become bigger than you are. Moreover, when people use what they have learned from you, your effect in this world is greatly magnified.

Another example of how this works comes from an acquaintance. Ashley became ill with an autoimmune disorder that left her exhausted, in pain, and unable to work. It took her many years to get the right diagnosis and she relied on an online support group of similarly disabled people. During that time, she educated herself on her disease and its underlying causes. Once she was finally diagnosed, she worked with her health team on a treatment plan that allowed her more flexibility in her life, and she was able to work part-time again. When a new person joined her online support group who had the same health issues as she did, Ashley reported to me later, her first reaction was to keep what she knew to herself. After all, she did years of research becoming an unacknowledged expert on her condition; why shouldn't this new person do the same? She realized right away that was wrong thinking. Why should someone else suffer as she had when she could help? She did a one-eighty and gave away the information that this new person was seeking. By doing so, she helped someone else and gave herself a new friend in return.

One note: There is a difference between giving away information that is wanted and needed and giving away unasked-for advice. It can be easy to create a false feeling of "giving away" when you tell other people how to do their jobs. A supervisor who constantly interferes or micromanages their workers is not giving away information. That kind of behavior often comes from a place of need to control, not from a sincere and positive desire to give.

Give Away Praise

For many of us, the people we find most difficult to praise are the ones closest to us—our partners, our children, our parents, and sometimes our friends. A lot of the difficulty comes from anger and resentment. Yet, in some strange way, when we praise the people in our lives, we release the negativity and open the door for their being loving toward us.

Too many in relationships focus on the negative and have no difficulty reminding significant others of what they are doing wrong. It is no wonder so few relationships are going well. We want our loved ones to be affirming and supportive. It is important to surround ourselves with giving, loving, and nurturing people. This implies the flip side of the coin:

. . .

You must become what you want to attract. Be the kind of person you would want to surround yourself with.

. . .

When we find ourselves wallowing in negativity, with a woe-is-me attitude, the last thing any of us need is to be surrounded by people who feel similarly. Yet how many of our friends belong to the Moan and Groan Society with us? As like attracts like, the only way to break free of our cycle of misery is to make a change. Giving away praise is a wonderful way to start. Does your spouse look wonderful in a new shirt? Tell them. Has your friend created a comfortable, cozy home? Tell them. Is your daughter's new hairstyle not really your thing, but you can see how she is proud of it? Tell her she looks happy.

Like giving away thanks and giving away attention, giving away praise costs us nothing and gives so much. You'll find that when you get in the habit of praising friends, colleagues, family, and even strangers, that praise in your honor will be more forthcoming.

One of the doubters in my class asked me what happens if you give and give and give and get nothing back. I asked her for an example. She said that she gave and gave and gave to a man with whom she was trying to reestablish a relationship, and he refused to come back to her. I think she missed the point. In the first place, she was hardly giving with no expectations. She was expecting a lot! By her own admission, she felt that if she continued to give, he would see what he was missing and would finally come back to her.

I pointed out that it seemed more like a calculated con job, rather than an act of love. I suggested that she needed to release him and move on to someone who could better fill her needs. I reminded her that there is nothing wrong with the giving, but if our needs are not being met in a relationship, it is time to close that door, *with love,* and move on to someone else. Giving does not imply becoming a doormat. We are entitled to have our needs met. However, it doesn't serve us to be angry if a certain someone does not fulfill them.

Give Away Time

Time is something there never seems to be enough of; hence it is one of our most valuable commodities. It is also one of our most precious gifts. How do you give away time? You listen to a friend's problem, you write a note of thanks, you get involved in something bigger than yourself and become a participating member, you volunteer, you read a book to a child, drive a friend to the doctor, help a coworker move house. All of these, and more, take you out of yourself and help you operate from a different part of your being—the part that is loving, nurturing, and abundant.

Elizabeth, a Black woman, fought tooth and nail to succeed in her career as a financial advisor, despite coworkers and bosses who created obstacles for her, wanting her to fail. Now that she's at the top of her game, she spends a number of hours each week working with young people and newcomers to her field, helping them to achieve their goals. Some of her colleagues wonder at the time she spends on her "side project." Elizabeth is happy to tell anyone that asks that she does it because no one was there for her when she could have used a helping hand. Giving away her time is how she recognizes the abundance in her life, shows her gratitude, and makes sure no one feels as alone as she did.

David, one of my students, talked about one of his experiences of giving away his time. He volunteered for the Holiday Project, which involved visiting hospitals at Christmastime. He described it as "an opening up" of his heart and taking it "out of the ordinary and petty into a different space . . . a high place." Notice what David was feeling from his contribution of time. He remembered singing to a child in a coma. The nurse had told him, "Sing to him . . . he'll hear you." He said it was beautiful and advised the rest of the class to open themselves up to such a contribution. "It's incredibly inspiring!"

A dear friend of mine who recently had a stroke felt blessed and abundant at Thanksgiving time. She volunteered, wheelchair and all, to help cook Thanksgiving dinner in a restaurant that was serving free meals to the unhoused. She loved every moment of it. She knows she counts, even after her stroke.

Volunteering is also a wonderful way to spend holidays with your own children. One of my friends was aghast when her daughter, after opening 52 presents, said, "Is that all?" That was the last of that kind of Christmas for her daughter. Now, each year she and her daughter are part of the Holiday Project that David talked about, and she has seen a transformation in her daughter. Instead of always wondering what she will be getting for Christmas, her daughter spends a lot of time creating things to take to the hospital and give away.

I want to say a word about volunteering in general. During my years at the Floating Hospital, I had many opportunities to observe volunteers. There were generally two categories: those who knew they counted and those who didn't. And what a difference there was between them!

The latter helped, not out of a sense of giving, but out of a sense of obligation: "I should be giving back to the community." Some of these used their volunteer experience as a way of proving to everyone else what "good" people they were. This is not to say that some were not of help. They were. Though some definitely were not! Their egos always got in the way. These were the ones who were not interested in what the Floating Hospital needed, but only in what would feed their egos. Hence, they often became more of a problem than a help to the staff. What was worse, they probably derived little sense of satisfaction or personal worth from their experience.

Those who knew they counted were a different breed entirely. They were there, silent but sure. They responded to our needs almost before we asked. They were diligent about being on time and never failed to show up when expected. They did anything required of them, no matter how menial it might have seemed. They did it with joy, knowing they were of use. They rarely talked about what they did—they just did it. And they were greatly loved for their contribution.

The difference between the way we operate in this world when we know we count and when we don't know we count is staggering. If you have not yet acknowledged that you count in this world, simply go around "acting as if" you do. Ask yourself, "If I really counted, what would I be doing in this situation? How would I be acting?" It really works.

So, knowing that you count, or "acting as if" you do, give away your time. What an incredible gift for you and others!

Give Away Money

Money is a huge challenge for most of us. I have worried about money since I was two years old. I always joke that God has made me this way on purpose because God was afraid I would be too lazy to write my books if I wasn't worried about money. No matter how successful I become, I have moments when I see myself at the age of 82, standing on the corner with a cup in my hand and begging for money. I have found that many have this image of themselves. Where this comes from I haven't the foggiest notion. I have never really wanted for anything in my whole life. Yet the fear persists.

Fear about money often endures regardless of how wealthy we are. I recently read a newspaper account of an immensely rich man who still has nightmares about losing everything. For him, enough will never be enough. Years ago I heard a great line in a B movie: "Security is not having money; it's knowing you can do without it." The fact that many of us have never been without money might be the problem. Here is another instance when a lack might have provided a very valuable lesson. The philosopher Seneca knew what he was talking about when he wrote so long ago, "Set aside a certain number of days, during which you shall be content with the scantiest and cheapest fare, with coarse and rough dress, saying to yourself the while: 'Is this the condition that I feared?'"

The answer to an obsession with money lies in loosening up and letting go. Within reason, begin to "give it away" with the belief that you will always find a way to have whatever you need. One friend of mine writes "thank you" on the checks with which she pays her bills. In this attitude, freedom lies—freedom to enjoy, to invest in yourself and others, and to be a creative part of the flow. Giving away money can pay off enormously in actual dollars brought in, but, more important, in peace of mind. This is not to say that you should squander your money—balance is the key.

Give Away Love

As far as I am concerned, all of the "giveaways" mentioned are about giving away love. But there are other ingredients in loving. For example, when we let someone be who they are without trying to change them, that is giving away love. When we trust that some-one can handle his or her own life, and act accordingly, that is giving away love. When we let go and allow others to learn and grow without feeling our existence is threatened, that is giving away love. How many relationships do you know that look like that?

What often looks like love is not—it is need. As stated by Rollo May in *Man's Search for Himself*, "Love is generally confused with dependence; but in point of fact, you can love only in pro-portion to your capacity for independence."

• • •

To love is to be able to give. And now is the time to begin.

• • •

I've discussed giving away thanks, praise, attention, informa-tion, time, money, and, now, love. I'm sure you can think of other things to add to the list. You now understand that giving is about outflow. It is about letting go of your crouched, withholding self and standing tall with outstretched arms. When we really feel this sense of abundance, we truly understand the saying "My cup runneth over."

Giving from the position that "I count" enhances your ability to give. Like any other skill, however, it takes practice.

Whether you presently believe it or not, your life is already abundant. You simply haven't noticed it. Before you can accept abundance in your life, you have to notice it.

Your Book of Abundance

One way to increase your awareness is through what I call The Book of Abundance. Buy yourself a beautiful notebook. If you prefer, you can create a computer document or use a notetaking app on your mobile phone. Start listing as many positive things in your life—past and present—as you can think of. Don't stop until you reach 150. Some of you will find more. When you feel you can't think of any more, you can. Just keep focusing on all the blessings in your life. No matter how small they seem, include them in your book.

Each day make entries in your book. Instead of a traditional journal—which for many is composed of doom and gloom, wish and want—create this Book of Abundance, which in effect simply states, "I have!" Note every positive thing, large or small, that happens—a compliment from a friend, a cheerful hello from the mail carrier, a beautiful sky, a chance to contribute, a haircut, a new suit, nourishing food. *Notice* everything wonderful that happens to you.

Use reminders to keep you focused "on the doughnut, not the hole." Look for blessings, and you will notice them all over the place. They will envelop you. There is so much you are not seeing that is already there. There is no need to feel scarcity when there is such abundance.

If you follow these directions, I suspect you will have a closet full of such books in a very short time. Refer to them often—especially when you are feeling a sense of lack. Lack is only in the mind. Some of the greatest givers I ever met were the impoverished at the Floating Hospital. I watched them and their sense of contribution to the people in their community, and it was joyous. Lack is not about money or things; it is about love. And love is always there for you to create when you are conscious that . . .

. . .

Your life is abundant, and you count!

. . .

In addition to your Book of Abundance, keep reading positive books, listening to motivational and inspirational audios, and repeating your affirmations. Say to yourself, "I RELEASE MY FEAR OF LACK AND ACCEPT THE ABUNDANCE AND PROSPERITY OF THE UNIVERSE," and whenever you feel fear relative to money, or anything else for that matter, repeat this affirmation. It will give you peace. It will also remind you of the abundance that exists in your life at any given moment.

Keep remembering that you are aiming to get to the point where you are the giver. When you are aware of the fact that "you have," you can give. When you are a giver, you have nothing to fear. You are powerful and you are loving. The trick in life is not figuring out what you can get, but what you can give. There is so much power in this kind of thinking that it staggers the imagination.

Think about this: if you see that your purpose in life is to give, then it's almost impossible to be taken advantage of. If someone takes, they are simply fulfilling your life's purpose, and they deserve your thanks. When you act the giving adult, your fears are diminished . . . you realize you are meant to be used.

George Bernard Shaw summed it up beautifully in the following quotation. Reading these words daily will greatly help you to put things in perspective and give you the courage to move beyond your fear, so that you can be of great use to the world:

This is the true joy in life, the being used for a purpose recognized by yourself as a mighty one, the being a force of nature instead of a feverish selfish little clod of ailments and grievances complaining that the world will not devote itself to making me happy.

I am of the opinion that my life belongs to the whole community and, as long as I live, it is my privilege to do for it whatever I can. I want to be thoroughly used up when I die, for the harder I work the more I live.

I rejoice in life for its own sake. Life is no brief candle to me. It is a sort of splendid torch which I've got to hold up for the moment and I want to make it burn as brightly as possible before handing it on to future generations.

11.

Filling the Inner Void

I have talked about a lot of powerful tools: affirmations, saying yes to your universe, positive thinking, taking responsibility, no-lose decisions, choosing love and trust, learning to give, and more. The reason these are powerful tools is that they open us to a place within, which, when tapped, allows us to feel "full-filled."

This place within has been given a multitude of names, some of which are the Higher Self, the Inner Self, the Superconscious, the Higher Conscious, and the God-self. I like the term Higher Self, simply because it implies that we can move above that part of us, the Lower Self, that dwells on the petty things that cause fear, hate, scarcity, and all other forms of negativity. It brings to mind a new plane of existence that has little to do with everyday upsets and struggle.

There is a body of psychologists who believe in the existence of the Higher Self and the influence it can exert upon the individual. Some refer to their work with the Higher Self as height psychology. Others refer to it as transpersonal psychology. There are also many educators and metaphysicians whose work encompasses the realm of the Higher Self.

They have proposed that this Higher Self is capable of a high degree of sensitivity and attunement to a harmonious flow within the universe. It is the container of many sublime virtues—creativity, intuition, trust, love, joy, inspiration, aspiration, caring, giving—everything we, in our heart of hearts, would like to experience.

Too many of us seem to be searching for something "out there" to make our lives complete. We feel alienated, lonely, and empty. No matter what we do or have, we never feel full-filled. This feeling of emptiness or intense loneliness is our clue that we are off course, and that we need to correct our direction. Often we think that the correction lies in a new partner, house, car, job, or whatever. Not so.

I believe that what all of us are really searching for is this divine essence within ourselves. When we are far from our Higher Self, we feel what Roberto Assagioli has so aptly called "Divine Homesickness." When you are feeling this sense of being lost, or off-course, the thing to do to find your way home again is simply to use the tools that will align you with your Higher Self—and thus allow the good feelings to flow once again.

You might ask, "Where has this Higher Self been hiding all my life?" We often hear the expression "mind, body, and spirit." It is used to define our whole being. Modern society has been primarily concerned with body and mind. The spirit part, which encompasses the Higher Self, has somehow gotten lost in the shuffle. So it is not surprising that we have focused almost totally on the intellectual and physical parts of ourselves. In fact, many of us haven't even been aware that we have a spiritual part.

Since I first wrote this book, many years ago, there has been a rise in spiritual consciousness with more and more people practicing yoga and meditation, or going to classes or workshops that deal with our Higher Self. Mindfulness is being practiced by individuals, businesses, and even beginning to be taught to small children. Yet for all this spiritual awakening, most of us are still taught, even encouraged, to be in touch only with our rational mind and our bodies. We often neglect this other important component of our self.

Add to that the fact that many people don't even like the word "spiritual." They tune out the minute it is mentioned. The reason is that they confuse "spiritual" with religion and God. For those who are not religious, the word "spiritual" puts them off.

The way I use this word should be acceptable to you whether you are religious or not. When I speak of the spiritual, I speak of the Higher Self, the place within that is loving, kind, abundant, joyful, and has all those other qualities I mentioned earlier. Believe me when I tell you that unless you consciously or unconsciously tap into that spiritual part within, you will experience perpetual discontent.

I am sure that every one of you has at times operated from the spiritual part of yourself without labeling it as that. Have you ever given something to someone and felt so good, it brought tears to your eyes? Have you ever been so overwhelmed with the beauty of something, a sunset or a flower, that you were filled with a sense of abundance? Have you ever looked beyond someone's ugly behavior and felt only love for them as you saw their pain? Have you ever cried tears of joy when moved by a movie or a song? If you did any of these things, it could be said you were operating from the Higher Self. You transcended the world of the petty—"They didn't even say thank you"; "They never pick up their dirty socks"; "Why don't they call more often?"—and touched a world of beauty beyond.

You experience an incredible high when your Personal Higher Self hooks into a Group Higher Self. If your heart swelled at the closing ceremonies of the Olympics—when you got a sense of how magnificent this world would be if we all acted as one for the good of all—you got a sense of the Group Higher Self. The power and love that can generate are phenomenal.

As you are undoubtedly aware, power, and even a sense of a high, can be generated by evil as well. The difference is the almost blissful feeling you get from all things generated by the Higher Self, which is inherently a loving space. Power from a negative place, or from our Lower Self, does not alleviate our Divine Homesickness. In fact, it takes us far, far from home. Thus, when the temporary sense of power leaves, you are left lost, lonely, and frightened. When you operate from the Higher Self, you feel centered and abundant—in fact, overflowing. When you experience this abundance, your fears disappear.

The Higher Self is also in operation when you create "miracles" in your life—the power to lift a car if a loved one is trapped underneath or the power to accomplish a monumental task that everyone has told you is impossible. I have often heard people say, "I don't know how I did it, but I did!" Their power came from their Higher Self.

Now that I've introduced you to your Higher Self, let me show you an ultrasimple model of being. The model on the following page is not comprehensive; it leaves out many parts of our internal and external worlds. It does serve, however, to remind us that we can choose our experiences of life.

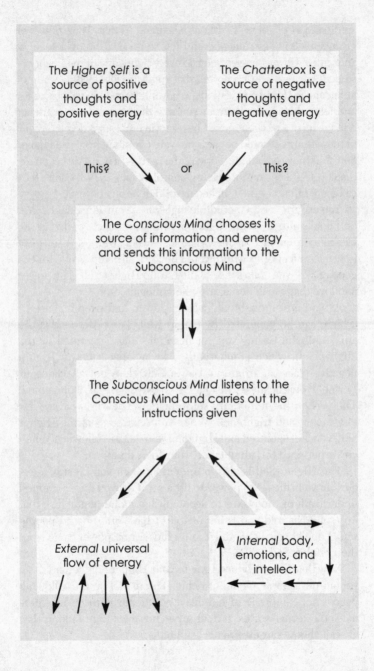

The *Higher Self* is a source of positive thoughts and positive energy

The *Chatterbox* is a source of negative thoughts and negative energy

This?   or   This?

The *Conscious Mind* chooses its source of information and energy and sends this information to the Subconscious Mind

The *Subconscious Mind* listens to the Conscious Mind and carries out the instructions given

External universal flow of energy

Internal body, emotions, and intellect

The Chatterbox, as you'll remember, is the part of us that tries to drive us crazy. It is the repository of all our negative input, from the time we were born to the present moment. In other words, it is our Lower Self—the exact opposite of our Higher Self. The Lower Self contains our childlike ego that needs constant attention and doesn't know how to give. The Conscious Mind sends orders to the Subconscious Mind based on the information it gets from either the Higher Self or the Chatterbox. We can train it to choose from either.

The Subconscious Mind is a storehouse of a huge amount of information. It operates in a computerlike fashion, sorting out and finding information. For example, when you can't remember a name, and suddenly, when you are least expecting it, it pops up out of nowhere. Your Subconscious Mind has been at work. The Subconscious Mind takes its orders from the Conscious Mind. It does not question or judge. It does not know right from wrong or healthy from unhealthy. Remember the arm experiment in Chapter 5. When the Subconscious Mind was told, "I am a strong and worthy person," the arm was strengthened. When it was told, "I am a weak and unworthy person," the arm was easily pushed down. The Subconscious Mind believes what the Conscious Mind tells it, whether or not it is true, or even whether you believe it or not.

As the model suggests, your mind can choose to listen to your Chatterbox blabbering away with all kinds of self-defeating negativity, or it can choose to listen to your Higher Self, which is self-affirming, loving, giving, and abundant. All of the exercises and concepts suggested in this book are geared toward having the Conscious Mind open its door to the abundance of the Higher Self as opposed to the scarcity of the Chatterbox, which comes directly from your Lower Self.

The Conscious Mind is often not aware that it is being run by the Chatterbox. And even if there is awareness, the Conscious Mind is so used to listening to the Chatterbox that, in the course of everyday events, it "forgets" to listen to the Higher Self and thus needs constant reminding. This is where the affirmations, positive thinking, audios, books, sayings, and whatever other tools you have come in handy—to remind your Conscious Mind that you do not have to listen to the Chatterbox any longer.

As with the Higher Self, the Chatterbox has always been there, and will always be there. No use lamenting the fact that it pops up every once in a while! I *guarantee* that it will. You must realize that you do have a Chatterbox within; and you have more, including the Higher Self. Neither one is right or wrong. Each simply gives you a different experience of life.

If you listen to the Chatterbox, your experience of life is fear-producing, and you stop yourself from expanding. If you listen to the Higher Self, your experience of life is joyful and abundant and devoid of fear. You, like everyone else, are an expert at listening to your Chatterbox. Your task is now to become an expert at listening to your Higher Self. Then true choice will be possible.

Why do so many positive things happen when the Conscious Mind chooses to operate from the Higher Self, and why does the reverse happen when it listens to the Chatterbox? It seems that when the Subconscious Mind receives its orders from the Conscious Mind, it seeks to carry them out by connecting internally to the body, intellect, and feelings. Thus, when it hears "I am a weak and unworthy person," it connects to your body and makes you physically weak. It connects to your feelings and makes you depressed and helpless. It connects to your intellect and makes you think stupidly. It also fills you with negative energy. When it hears "I am a strong and worthy person," it connects to your body and makes you strong. It connects to your feelings and makes you feel confident and alive. It connects to your intellect and makes you think clearly. It also fills you with positive energy.

What is more, outside yourself is a Universal Energy without which the world would not exist. In carrying out its orders, the energy of the Subconscious Mind connects to this Universal Energy, which manages to bring back exactly what you have "asked" for. If you put out "I am a weak and unworthy person," the universe obliges the Subconscious Mind and delivers all sorts of negative things. People step on you. You never achieve anything you want. Everything stands in your way, and you feel powerless to move anything aside.

When you put out "I am a strong and worthy person," the universe obliges the Subconscious Mind and delivers all sorts of positive things. People respect your strength and treat you fairly. You attain all sorts of wonderful things. Nothing stands in your way as you find the means to remove any obstacles. The key here is that just as your Subconscious Mind does not judge, neither does the Universal Energy.

Metaphysicians talk about Laws of Universal Energy. One of these is the Law of Attraction. You've probably heard or read about this already, as there have been several popular books on the subject recently. You will recognize the Law of Attraction as "like attracts like." When you send out negative energy, what will you attract? Negative energy. When you send out positive energy, what will you attract? Positive energy. Perhaps this makes clearer why it is imperative to train your mind to send out only positive thoughts.

Some of you might have trouble accepting the idea of Universal Energy. You don't need to believe this concept in order to tap into your Higher Self. However, when you can see yourself connected to something bigger than yourself, you no longer feel you must do it all alone. Your sense of power becomes highly magnified, and your fears are greatly diminished. This relates back to the Level 3 Fear: "I'm afraid I can't handle it." Now you can see that with the Universal Energy on your side, you can learn to trust not only yourself, but the universe as well. This kind of dual trust ultimately signals the end of fear.

One of the tools the Subconscious Mind uses to connect you with what you are looking for is your *intuition*. Those strange messages you get are the Subconscious Mind saying, "I found it!" Anyone who has experienced the power of intuition cannot deny that something is acting on our behalf if we listen to it. By learning to trust your intuition, "miracles" seem to happen.

Our intuition is always operating for us—usually, however, we don't act on it. When I made the conscious decision to start acting on thoughts that were coming through my head, amazing "coincidences" began to occur. My original "fear class" came about as a result of my intuition. At the time, I had a vague notion that one day in the future I wanted to teach a course on fear. I put it off indefinitely, largely because I was too busy with other things to write up the course description and outline and then find a school that would want me to teach such a course. It seemed like a lot of work.

One day, as I sat at my desk working, a strong message came to mind. It said, "Go to the New School for Social Research." I couldn't figure out why this message came into my head. I never attended the New School; I knew no one there. In fact, I didn't even know where it was. Out of curiosity, I decided to go. I told my assistant I was going to the New School, and she asked why. I said, "I don't know!" She looked at me strangely as I walked out the door.

I got into a taxi that delivered me right to the door of the New School. When I walked into the lobby, I asked myself, "What should I do now?" I saw a directory and looked at the various departments listed. My eye caught on Human Relations. "That's where I'm supposed to go." My mind reasoned that I was probably "sent" here to sign up for a great workshop they were offering. I was a workshop addict at the time. The idea of teaching at the New School didn't occur to me.

I found the door marked Human Relations Department and walked inside. No one was at the reception desk. I looked through the door on my right and saw a woman sitting at her desk. She called out, "Can I help you?" Intuitively, without "thinking" about it, I surprised myself by saying, "I'm here to teach a course about overcoming fear." Without my realizing it, I was talking to the head of the department, a wonderful woman named Ruth Van Doren. She looked at me with amazement and finally blurted out, "I can't believe that! I've been searching high and low for someone to teach a course about fear, and haven't been able to find anyone. And today is my deadline—all catalog descriptions must be in today."

She inquired about my credentials and was pleased with them. She then told me she had to run to catch a bus and asked me to quickly write up a course description with a course title. I did. She handed it to her assistant and ran out the door, thanking me profusely.

After she left, I stood in a state of shock. I had had no conscious intention of proposing a course that day. And what I had imagined would be an arduous task, taking months, took exactly twelve minutes! Ruth Van Doren wanted something, I wanted something, and the universe put us together. How this works, I don't know. I simply know it works. The amazing thing is that, had I consciously thought it through, I would never have approached the New School. I would have gone to Hunter College, where I went to undergraduate school, or to Columbia University, where I had obtained my advanced degrees. I knew a lot of people in both places. The New School would not have entered my Conscious Mind.

It is worth noting that teaching that course was a turning point in my life. My experience was so positive and felt so "right" that I decided to leave my job of ten years to become an educator and writer. Oh, by the way, you might have guessed the course title I chose. It was "Feel the Fear and Do It Anyway"!

I'm sure you have heard of even more dramatic examples of the working of intuition—lives being saved, people getting together despite tremendous odds, and other amazing happenings. The point is that we all have access to this intuitive power simply by starting to listen to the messages the Subconscious Mind is telling us. I suspect it works on instructions we have given it when we are clearly unaware we are doing so. We might have forgotten about it, but the subconscious never forgets. In fact, it works better when we take our Conscious Mind off the issue and let it do its work without our interference. That is why we get some of our most inspired ideas when we are relaxing or doing something other than the task that needs a solution.

Simply start paying attention to what you are being told and then act on it. If the mind says, "Call so and so," call them. If it says, "Go here," go here. If it says "Go there," go there. In the beginning you may be confused about whether it is your intuition operating or your Chatterbox or whatever. Just keep following the instructions, and soon you will be able to tell the difference. I'm at the point where I act on most of these seemingly "stray" thoughts that enter my mind, and I am amazed at the connections that have been made.

TAPPING INTO YOUR INTUITION

In *Embracing Uncertainty*, I devote an entire chapter to increasing the power of the intuitive part of who we are. There are a number of books, classes, and videos that focus on developing the intuitive mind, but let me give you some guidance about how to get started. Here are a number of steps you can take to start practicing right now.

1. *Focus on Your Highest Good:* Rather than focus on your plans for your life, trust that the Grand Design has its own plans for you.

2. *Quiet the Mind:* Stop thinking and worrying about a problem and allow yourself to just "know" the solution. When we stop the Chatterbox and trust, often our Subconscious Mind will already have the answer waiting.

3. *Stop Being a Know-It-All:* When we think we know all the answers, we become rigid and unbending. Intuition is something that flows, but we can't flow with it if we have our minds made up.

4. *Create "Intention":* Knowing what you want, what you *really* want, sends radio waves to the Universal Energy, which helps get you where you need to be. A strong intention can have amazing results.

5. *Turn the Questions Over to Your Subconscious Mind:* This means that when you are experiencing indecision or confusion, allow your Subconscious Mind to deal with it. You can even say, "Subconscious Mind, take over please!" *Then get out of your own way.* The answer will come to you often when it is least expected.

6. *Listen to the Whispers:* Only with a quiet mind can you hear the "whispers." When the Chatterbox is quiet we can learn to focus on the "gap between our thoughts," allowing the intuitive answers to come.

7. *Take Action on Your Intuitive Thoughts:* When a whispered command comes into your thoughts, act on it. If you get the urge to call a friend, do it. If an opportunity presents itself to you, welcome it. Take action and move forward.

8. *Don't Analyze:* If you allow your rational mind to get involved in the process, it will be easy to discount what the Universal Energy is telling you. Act purely on inner trust.

9. ***Practice, Practice, Practice:*** You won't get anywhere with your intuition if you aren't willing to put in the effort to hear it. Like so many things, this may not come easily. You must practice listening to your intuition until you hear it clearly, and then following it more naturally will become part of who you are.

I have begun to rely so much on my Subconscious Mind that when I am troubled by something, I simply say, "I ask my Subconscious Mind to find the solution for me." I then stop worrying and thinking about it. Somehow, easily and effortlessly, the solution comes. A particularly effective time to do this is as you go off to sleep at night. Simply let go and turn it over. You'll probably sleep much better as a result. And you might surprise yourself with the result when you wake up!

When you are upset, you are not letting in the abundance of the Higher Self. If you are aligned or "centered" as illustrated here, you feel yourself in a harmonious flow.

When you stay centered there is nothing to fear. You are tapping your source of power, and everything is okay. But how can you become centered, especially when you are upset?

If you are particularly rattled about something—let's say about getting a job you desperately want—the anxiety begins to build. You begin to feel that if that job isn't offered, your world will fall apart. The Chatterbox takes over and begins to drive you crazy, convincing you that it is the only job out there, and without it you will not survive. The Chatterbox is pulling you off center. It is then that you begin to use the techniques presented in this book.

You start to repeat your affirmations. You begin using your Pain-to-Power Vocabulary to put it in perspective. You put on calming music or a guided meditation or an affirmation audio. You begin to tap into your source of power—that place within where you can see the world as a safe and nourishing place. Keep remembering that it is just as realistic to think positively as negatively. And also remember the arm experiment. Positive self-talk works even if you don't believe it initially.

Say to yourself:

"This job is not my life. If I do not get it, it is because it is not for my highest good. If I am meant to have it, it will be mine. I can relax now and turn it over to my Subconscious Mind and the Universal Energy out there. All the answers I need are within me. It is all happening perfectly. There is nothing to fear."

While you are telling yourself these truths, work on relaxing your body. If you continue to feed yourself these affirming words long enough, you will eventually notice a warm calm come over your body and your mind and you will feel safe. Each positive statement pulls you, like a magnet, closer to the center . . . to your source. You've come to the place where all is safe. You've let go of the outcome, and there is nothing to fear.

It may take a while in the beginning to pull back to the center. So find yourself a quiet space and sit there for as long as it takes to make you feel better. Your calming background audio really helps get you to align faster. Not only does it set the mood and block out extraneous noise, but it also eventually conditions you to relax and feel your power the minute you turn it on.

What could you tell yourself if the problem is not your job, but your relationship?

"This person is not my life. If we are meant to be together, we will be. If not, so be it. I trust that my Subconscious Mind and the Universal Energy are creating the perfect relationship for me. I can let go trusting that everything is happening perfectly. My life is full. My life is rich. There is nothing to fear."

Early in our marriage, my husband and I found a perfect house for us. It was more than we were prepared to pay; nevertheless, we put in a bid. I found myself beginning to be obsessed about having the house. The Chatterbox began:

"You'll never find the money for the down payment. If you sell your assets, you won't have anything to draw on. And what if you need money? If you lose that house, there will be no others out there as beautiful. But how are we ever going to raise the money?"

I quickly sat myself down and began the positive self-talk that would magnetize me back to the center.

"This house is not my life. If I am meant to have it, it will be mine, and the money will come to us easily and effortlessly. If it is not the house for us, we will find another one just as beautiful, perhaps more so. I'm turning it over to my Subconscious Mind to give me all the answers I need to know. It is all happening perfectly. There is nothing to fear."

All my obsessiveness stopped, and a warm calm came over me. Each time I felt myself listening to the Chatterbox, I returned to that place of safety and calm. The house was meant to be ours because the money did come to us easily and effortlessly. By trusting the universe I could feel myself drawing toward me all that I needed to handle the purchase of the house comfortably.

I am convinced that:

. . .

**If we do not consciously and
consistently focus on the spiritual part
of ourselves, we will never experience
the kind of joy, satisfaction, safety, and
connectedness we are all seeking.**

. . .

It takes practice. When people speak of "being on the path"
or of life as a "journey," they are referring to the constant vigil required to train the Conscious Mind to listen to the lessons of the
Higher Self, which, because of interference from the Chatterbox,
elude us at times.

Let's go back and see how using your Whole Life Grid can provide the practice you need. I suggest that one of your permanent
boxes be the Higher Self. Each day incorporate time to be quiet
and to focus on the Higher Self, using the various tools suggested—
affirmations, inspirational audios, meditation, or whatever works
for you. The best time to do this is in the morning, because it sets
up the entire day. Focus on the Higher Self area of the grid before
you go to bed as well—perhaps instructing your Higher Self to find
the answer to some problem you may be encountering.

The Higher Self box is different from all the others because it
is the one area of the grid that positively influences every other
area of your life. It is from this higher place, above the petty, that
you create value wherever you go and in whatever you do. Coming thus from a spiritual place, you enhance the quality of your
relationship with the rest of the world—family, work, contribution, friends, personal growth, and so on. Keeping this in mind,
your grid would look like the one shown opposite.

The positive, loving energy that flows from a heightened spiritual-
ity will spill over into every area of your life. Those of you who have
already discovered your spiritual selves understand what I am talking
about. And for those of you who haven't, you have a real treat in store.

The Contribution box can serve to keep you aligned. When
you become involved in a bigger energy motivated by the Group

Higher Self, you are infused with power and purpose. It helps to contribute to something you believe in with all your heart. Make Contribution a permanent box in your grid as well. It will serve to remind you that you have so much to give, even if you don't think you do. Remember, "act as if" works whether you believe it or not.

Whole Life with Spirituality

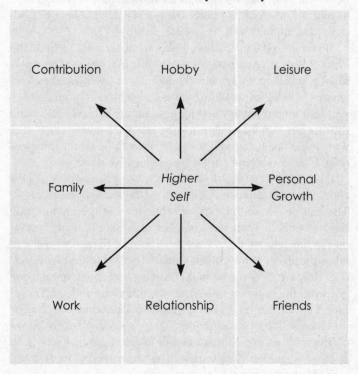

It is not the purpose of this book to explain the world of the spiritual. What I hope to do, however, is whet your appetite, so you will be eager to learn more. I urge you to look at the laws of the universe as postulated by metaphysicians. I gave you only one; there are many others. Don't let the word "metaphysics" put you off. It simply means the study of what is beyond the physical.

Metaphysical laws are amazingly simple to understand and can clear up many confusions about the way the world works. They can help you create a much greater trust in yourself and trust in the universe—which, of course, is the antidote to fear. These laws take a lifetime of practice, as does everything else in this book, but they will give you a sense of the direction in which you should be heading. For those of you who are religious and/or believe in God, you will see how these ideas can be incorporated in your beliefs. And, as I said earlier, if you don't believe in God, these laws apply as well.

If you have the inclination, I also encourage you to study the ideas of Roberto Assagioli, a great thinker in the area of transpersonal psychology. Assagioli is the founder of psychosynthesis, an amazing model for self-integration and self-realization. Psychosynthesis employs many techniques that are valuable in freeing us from past conditioning, resolving internal conflicts (such as "I want to be taken care of" versus "I want to be totally independent"), and awakening our loving and creative powers.

One of the powerful tools used by the practitioners of psychosynthesis and other disciplines is the *guided visualization*. This can be one of the most effective ways of quickly touching the Higher Self. There are a number of wonderful books written on the subject, and again I suggest you read them. But really to know the power of the guided visualization, you must experience one. Reading gives you an understanding, but going through one gives you the experience—a dramatic difference indeed. Therefore, I encourage you to take a guided visualization workshop or purchase audios of visualizations. There are also plenty of places on the internet and through mobile phone apps that offer free or low-cost guided visualizations. (Just be sure you research the source before purchasing.)

In brief, a guided visualization requires that you close your eyes, relax your body, and listen to the person giving you instructions. It uses the power of your imagination to see life as it would be seen if you listened only to your Higher Self. If you are fearful, your imagination is plugged into the Chatterbox, and often the only things you can conjure up are horror stories. With guided visualizations you can learn to push aside the Chatterbox for a moment and experience feelings and see mental pictures the likes of which you have never felt or seen before. The pictures are often of such beauty, you will be moved to tears of joy. Even negative pictures that arise are valuable; they often reveal insights you have been hiding from yourself.

There are those who have difficulty creating visual pictures, and for them guided visualizations are not effective. If you are one of these people, don't worry: simply use the other tools, such as affirmations, to help you find your way into the Higher Self. I do suggest, however, that you give visualizations a try.

It can be very effective to read aloud the visualizations given in books into a voice recording application or software, using as soothing a voice as you can project. By listening to visualization tapes by others, you will get a sense of the timing required between sentences to produce the full effect.

The following is a shortened version of a guided visualization my Feel the Fear and Do It Anyway workshop trainers and I use in my classes, which is also found on my audio *The Art of Fearbusting*.

Sit in a comfortable chair, with back straight, feet on the ground, hands comfortably on your lap. You have nothing to do but listen to my instructions and let whatever comes up for you come up. There is no right or wrong way to do a visualization. Just accept whatever comes up for you.

Now close your eyes . . . and keep them closed throughout the visualization. Take a deep breath . . . inhale all the loving energy in the universe . . . and exhale all your loving energy into the universe . . . Once more . . . in . . . and out . . . And once more . . . in . . . and . . . out. Feel how good it feels to begin to totally relax. Begin at the top of your head and work your way down to your feet . . . relax. Let go of the muscles . . . between your eyes . . . in your cheeks . . . mouth . . . neck . . . shoulders . . . back . . . arms . . . hands . . . chest . . . stomach . . . buttocks . . . legs . . . feet . . . Just totally let go . . . checking out any part of your body that may still be holding tension . . . and release it . . . Now I

*want you to think of a goal that you have in life . . . a
specific goal . . . and you know that fear is keeping you
from moving forward toward that goal . . . Now what
I'd like you to do is to imagine yourself approaching
that goal "as if" you had no fear . . . I want you to see
yourself approaching that goal with a sense of power
and confidence in yourself . . . confidence that it will
all be all right . . . What would you be doing . . . if
you had no fear? . . . See yourself . . . What would
you be doing next . . . if you had no fear? . . .*

*Look at the people around you . . . How are you
relating to them . . . with no fear? . . . How are they
relating to you? . . . Just enjoy this sense of power
and notice your ability to love . . . and contribute . . .
And know that this is a feeling always within you . . .
always a part of you . . . And it is within your capability
to move forward in life with that power and with
that confidence . . . See yourself . . . actualizing your
goal . . . with your power . . . with your confidence . . .
with your love . . . and with your contribution.*

*And slowly . . . start to bring yourself back to this
room . . . knowing that that power is available to you . . .
As soon as you begin to act . . . the power will come
forward. Feel yourself in your chair . . . be present in this
room . . . listen to the sounds around you . . . and when
you are ready, open your eyes . . . no need to rush. When
you are ready, open your eyes. Stretch and just feel the
deliciousness of your power. It's all there for the taking.*

You, or a friend with a soothing voice, could speak this visualization into a voice recorder, on your computer or mobile phone,
leaving ample space between each instruction to allow your imagination to create detail and feeling in the various scenes.

For those in my classes and my Feel the Fear and Do It Anyway workshops who tune in to visualizations, this one is very powerful. Many reported that for the first time they were able to see
what the world looks like without fear. They reported that when
they took away the fear, they were left with an abundance of love.

They were startled by how beautiful the world appeared and how much they wanted to give to the people around them. If you have no concept of how the world can look without fear, it is hard to know what you are striving for. Once that vision is revealed to you, the Path is much easier to follow. You know when you are tuning in to the Higher Self and when you aren't.

Visualizations can also be used to find answers to questions about the meaning and purpose of your life, or to clarify your life goals, or to reveal important truths you hide from yourself. They have a multitude of applications and offer incredible insights—so much so that they are valuable tools used by educators and therapists.

I've presented you with a lot of ideas and a lot of tools, but to have them work effectively requires your trust. I've often been asked to prove that all I teach is true. I can only answer that certain things are not provable—at least not yet.

I can't prove that a Higher Self exists. I can't prove that we are connected to a wonderful source of healing, nurturing energy. I can't prove that the Subconscious Mind can create "miracles" in both the inside and outside world. I can't prove that the tools I've given you work. But I do know that when I use these concepts as the model for my life, my experiences are transformed and I find myself absolutely in love with life and everything that it entails—all of it. I can't prove I am right . . . *nor can anyone prove I am wrong*. As Hugh Prather wrote in *There Is a Place Where You Are Not Alone*:

. . .

Why choose to be right instead of happy when there is no way to be right?

. . .

Having experienced life from the vantage point of both the Chatterbox and the Higher Self, my choice is the latter. I will do whatever it takes to open myself up more and more to a mind and heart filled with love, joy, creativity, satisfaction, and peace. That is my goal and, having used the techniques in this book, I have traveled many miles toward that goal. It is a lifelong process and one that I'm sure will bring much happiness into your life.

THE CHOICE IS MINE

When I am tuned in to my Chatterbox	*When I am tuned in to my Higher Self*
I try to control	I trust
I don't notice my blessings	I appreciate
I need	I love
I am insensitive	I care
I am in turmoil	I am at peace
I am blocked	I am creative
I don't know I count	I count
I repel	I attract
I make a – difference	I make a + difference
I take	I give and receive
I am bored	I am involved
I am empty	I am filled up
I am filled with self-doubt	I am confident
I am dissatisfied	I am content
I have tunnel vision	I see big
I wait and wait	I live now
I am helpless	I am helpful
I never enjoy	I am joyful
I am always disappointed	I go with what is
I hold resentment	I forgive
I am tense	I am relaxed
I am a robot	I am alive
I am being passed by	I love getting older
I am weak	I am powerful
I am vulnerable	I am protected
I am off course	I am on the path
I try to control	I let go
I am poor	I have so much
I am lonely	I am connected
I am afraid	*I am excited*

it's all happening perfectly it's all happening perfectly

12.

There Is Plenty of Time

it's all happening perfectly it's all happening perfectly

There you sit . . . filled with all sorts of information about how to make yourself powerful in the face of all your fears. What's next? What can I say to help keep you on course as you continue on the next part of your journey? First, the encouragement and motivation you have already received from this book will always be here for you whenever you need it. When you feel you are going off course or are being battered about by outside forces, come back and reread the parts that make you feel good.

Also, since *Feel the Fear . . . and Do It Anyway* was originally published, I have written *Feel the Fear . . . and Beyond* to give you practice using the exercises you have learned in this book. The more practice, the better!

The biggest pitfall as you make your way through life is impatience. Remember that being impatient is simply a way of punishing yourself. It creates stress, dissatisfaction, and fear. Whenever your Chatterbox is making you feel impatient, ask it, "What's the rush? It's all happening perfectly. Don't worry. When I am ready to move forward, I will. In the meantime, I am taking it all in and I am learning."

When we wake up to the potential power within, our impulse is to grab it all "quick." The more we grab, the more it seems to elude us. There is no quick. There are quick—and wonderful—seminars, workshops, books, and audios that give you tools, but they are not quick solutions. They are to be used and mastered throughout a lifetime.

I liken our impatience to an incident with my son when he was a little boy. I showed him how to plant a seed in a flowerpot and explained that soon, from the little seed, a beautiful flower would appear. I left him with his flowerpot and went on to do other things. Much later I returned to his room and saw he had placed a chair in front of the flowerpot and was sitting there watching it. I asked him what he was doing, and he said, "I'm waiting for the flower to appear." I realized I had neglected something in my explanation. So don't let me do the same thing to you.

So often when we are discouraged and think that we are learning nothing from all our efforts, changes are really taking place within us. We become aware of them long after they have been going on. Ultimately, my son did have his flower. One day he awoke and it was there. Although it didn't look like anything was happening, it was. And so it is with you.

One day, I threw a log on the smoldering embers of a dying fire and returned to the book I was reading. From time to time, I'd glance over at the fire and notice that there was no flame yet. There wasn't even the smoke that often signals a fire to come. Then, as I stared at the seemingly dead fire, flames suddenly burst out around the log. Patience means knowing it will happen . . . and giving it time to happen.

Again, it requires TRUST—trust that it is all happening perfectly. What do I mean by "perfectly"? I have come to believe there are only two kinds of experiences in life: those that stem from our Higher Self and those that have something to teach us. We recognize the first as pure joy and the latter as struggle. But they are both perfect. Each time we confront some intense difficulty, we know there is something we haven't learned yet, and the universe is now giving us the opportunity to learn. If we go through the experience with this in mind, all the "victim" is taken out of the situation, and we allow ourselves to say YES. Thus, no matter what is happening at any particular time in your life, keep in mind that it is all perfect.

As long as you can remember that life is an ongoing process of learning, you won't have the disgruntling sense that you haven't made it yet. My experience has shown me that so much of the joy in life is the challenge of figuring it out. Nothing is as satisfying as those moments of breakthrough when you discover something about yourself and the universe that adds another piece to the jigsaw puzzle. The joy of discovery is delicious. I know of no explorer who once having reached his or her goal has not wanted to go out and explore some more.

The challenge is to stay on the Path of the Higher Self. It is a far more enjoyable journey than the other paths you may choose to follow. You will know if you are on the right path by the way you feel. Trust your feelings. If the path you're on isn't providing you joy, satisfaction, creativity, love, and caring, that's not it. Say to yourself, "Okay, I tried this, and this isn't it. What else can I try?" Don't be deceived into thinking that by changing the external, the internal will be changed. It works the other way around.

The path that needs changing is the one in your mind. This is not to say that once you become aligned with your Higher Self, you won't want to change things in your physical world, but it is your mind that has to be changed first—then all that is right will follow.

The Path is much like the experience of climbing a mountain. The climb is tough. But each time you stop to look around, the view becomes more spectacular. You see a greater expanse, and the "flaws" of the world below disappear as you see more and more of the whole. As you climb higher, you are detached from the heaviness below. You feel lighter. You feel freer. And you are propelled higher by the increasing beauty you see.

From this vantage point, you become more compassionate as well. You may dislike some individuals intensely for their cruel behavior. But from a higher place, you'll see more of the whole. These individuals are more than their "flawed" behavior. They, too, have a magnificent interior place, which they haven't discovered yet. Hence you'll begin to feel their sadness and not be so harsh in your judgment.

This "higher place" perspective resembles the Overview Effect, a concept described by Frank White in his book *The Overview Effect—Space Exploration and Human Evolution*. White tells us that some astronauts report a cognitive shift in awareness from the experience of viewing Earth from outer space, where there are no discernible national boundaries or borders, and conflicts between nations and among individuals are invisible. These astronauts experience the feeling of a cosmic connection and a profound understanding that all of humanity and each individual are interconnected and synergistic.

Our journey upward on the Path of the Higher Self is not always a steady climb. You may climb, then stop and rest, regroup. So, too, with the spiritual journey. Sometimes it may seem as though you have stopped growing. Not so. You are just consolidating your information. You are refining your perspective and reaching your own version of the Overview Effect.

Some of what you learn may require that you drop beliefs and behavior that have been part of you from the time you were born. Sometimes you'll experience an *aha!* and transformation will seem instant. Again, not so. Sudden insights are the result of all that has happened before. Your Subconscious Mind, like a computer, searches and sorts without your awareness and, when you least expect it, comes up with the answer. Insights happen more frequently, however, the farther along the journey you are. The Conscious Mind lets go of its resistance to new ways of thinking. It develops more trust. The initial stages are the most difficult and require the greatest concentration.

Sometimes when you think you've finally "got it," the universe will step in to show you haven't. I've adopted a phrase of the performer Lena Horne's that keeps me humble: "I've come a long way . . . maybe!" I have learned that there is always more to learn. And experience is our greatest teacher.

That is why I am so in love with the aging process. Youth so rarely understands what age allows us to know. We need to go through many life experiences before the power within is brought forward in all its glory. And as long as we see ourselves as unfolding beings, there is no wish to go back one single day—and age becomes a beautiful thing.

One of my favorite passages reflecting the agony and ecstasy of our journey is from *The Velveteen Rabbit* by Margery Williams. In the story, two nursery toys, the Skin Horse and the Rabbit, talk about becoming Real:

> *"Does it hurt?" asked the Rabbit.*
>
> *"Sometimes," said the Skin Horse, for he was always truthful. "When you are Real, you don't mind being hurt."*
>
> *"Does it happen all at once, like being wound up," he asked, "or bit by bit?"*

*"It doesn't happen all at once," said the Skin Horse.
"You become. It takes a long time. That's why it doesn't
often happen to people who break easily, or have sharp
edges, or who have to be carefully kept. Generally,
by the time you are Real, most of your hair has been
loved off, and your eyes drop out and you get loose
in the joints and very shabby. But these things don't
matter at all, because once you are Real you can't
be ugly, except to people who don't understand."*

There is so much excitement and wonder in front of you. Sometimes you will experience the ecstasy of being in the flow. Sometimes you will experience the agony of being way off course. Remember you are not alone. This is a world filled with an abundance of support systems that are there for the taking whenever you are feeling troubled by life's experiences. One of my students said to me, "I read and read, and I assume one day one of those books is going to take!" I shot back, "No. *Nothing is going to take unless you take it!!*" And so it is with this book and every source available to you. DON'T WAIT FOR IT TO TAKE! TAKE IT! Use it. Live it. Absorb it. Unless you use the muscle that lifts you to your Higher Self, it will weaken—just as your body weakens when it is not used. If you think you need additional help, then by all means, enlist the aid of a professional. Take action. Nothing is going to work for you unless you do the work.

Say yes to life. Participate. Move. Act. Write. Read. Sign up. Take a stand. Or do whatever it takes for you. As Colette, the prolific French author, famously said, "No one asked you to be happy. Get to work!" Get involved in the process. *To become involved is to reduce our fear.* We become bigger, we move away from that "feverish, selfish little clod of ailments and grievances complaining that the world will not devote itself to making [us] happy." We move into true adult status, where we have much to give to this world.

As Rollo May wrote in *Man's Search for Himself*: "Every organism has one and only one central need in life, to fulfill its own potentialities." He goes on to say that joy is the result of using our powers to their fullest, and for that reason, joy, not happiness, is the goal of life.

And what is joy? It is something that expresses the ebullience of the spiritual part of ourselves. Joy is characterized by lightness, humor, laughter, and gaiety. Lighten up. If you have ever been around a person who is centered and enlightened, you are struck with their humor and ability to laugh at themselves. All the brittleness is gone and only fluidity remains.

So commit! Commit yourself to pushing through the fear and becoming more than you are at the present moment. The you that could be is absolutely colossal. You don't need to change what you are doing—simply commit to learning how to bring to whatever you do in life the loving and powerful energy of your Higher Self. Whether you are a bank teller, housewife or house-husband, corporate executive, student, assistant, janitor, teacher, programmer, salesperson, lawyer, scientist, or whatever, it's yours to give. As you live this way, moment by moment, day by day, in perfect time, you will find yourself moving closer and closer to Home. The paradox is that when you stay close to Home, you can go anywhere and do anything without fear. The Divine Homesickness disappears as you find the place where we all are connected as loving human beings. Whatever it takes to get you there, FEEL THE FEAR . . . AND DO IT ANYWAY!

Bibliography

Most of the following books and audios were in my head and heart when this book was published in 1987. I've included a few more recent resources that I thought you would find useful. Enjoy!

Assagioli, Roberto, *Psychosynthesis: A Collection of Basic Writings*. Amherst, MA: The Synthesis Center, Inc., 2012.

Bolen, Jean Shinoda, *The Tao of Psychology: Synchronicity and the Self*. San Francisco: HarperSanFrancisco, 1982, 2005.

Brown, Brené, *Daring Greatly: How the Courage to Be Vulnerable Transforms the Way We Live, Love, Parent, and Lead*. New York: Avery, 2012.

Canfield, Jack, *The Success Principles™: How to Get from Where You Are to Where You Want to Be*, 10th anniversary ed. Boston, MA: Mariner Books, 2015.

Chopra, Deepak, *The Spontaneous Fulfillment of Desire: Harnessing the Infinite Power of Coincidence*. New York: Harmony, 2003.

Cousins, Norman, *Anatomy of an Illness as Perceived by the Patient*, 20th anniversary ed. New York: W. W. Norton & Company, 2005.

Dobson, Terry, and Victor Miller, *Aikido in Everyday Life: Giving in to Get Your Way*. Berkeley, CA: North Atlantic Books, 1993.

Emery, Stewart, *Actualizations*. Garden City, NY: Dolphin Books, Doubleday and Company, 1977, 1978.

Ferguson, Marilyn, *The Aquarian Conspiracy: Personal and Social Transformation in Our Time*. Los Angeles: J. P. Tarcher, 2009.

Ferrucci, Piero, *What We May Be: The Visions and Techniques of Psychosynthesis*. Los Angeles: Tarcher Publishing, 1982, 2004.

Fields, Rick, with Peggy Taylor, Rex Weyler, and Rick Ingrasci, *Chop Wood, Carry Water: A Guide to Finding Spiritual Fulfillment in Everyday Life*. Los Angeles: J. P. Tarcher, 1984.

The Foundation for Inner Peace, *A Course in Miracles*. Tiburon, CA, 1975.

Frankl, Viktor, *Man's Search for Meaning*. Boston, MA: Beacon Press, n.d.

Gawain, Shakti, *Creative Visualization*, 40th anniversary ed. San Francisco, CA: New World Library, 2016.

———, *Living in the Light: Follow Your Inner Guidance to Create a New Life and a New World*. San Francisco, CA: New World Library, 2011.

Hay, Louise, *You Can Heal Your Life*. Carlsbad, CA: Hay House, 1984.

Hill, Napoleon, and W. Clement Stone, *Success Through a Positive Mental Attitude*. New York: Pocket Books, 1960.

Holden, Robert, *Shift Happens!: Powerful Ways to Transform Your Life*. Hay House Inc.; Revised edition (September 1, 2011).

Jampolsky, Gerald, *Love Is Letting Go of Fear*. Millbrae, CA: Celestial Arts, 1979, 2010.

Jeffers, Susan, *The Art of Fearbusting*. P.O. Box 5338, Santa Monica, CA 90409: Jeffers Press, 2005. (1-hour CD—A live talk)

———, *Embracing Uncertainty: Breakthrough Methods for Achieving Peace of Mind When Facing the Unknown*. New York: St. Martin's Press, 2003.

———, *End the Struggle and Dance with Life: How to Build Yourself Up When the World Gets You Down*. New York: St. Martin's Press, 1996.

———, *The Fear-Less Series: Inner Talk for Peace of Mind, Inner Talk for a Confident Day, Inner Talk for a Love That Works*. P.O. Box 5338, Santa Monica, CA 90409: Jeffers Press, 2005. www.jefferspress.com. (3 Affirmation CDs)

———, *Feel the Fear . . . and Beyond, Mastering the Techniques for Doing It Anyway*. A Fawcett Columbine Book, New York: Ballantine, 1998. www.randomhouse.com

———, *Feel the Fear . . . and Do It Anyway*. Carlsbad, CA: Hay House, 1992. (Unabridged 4-CD set)

———, *Feel the Fear . . . and Do It Anyway*. A Nightingale Conant

Production, A Simon & Schuster Audio, New York, 2001. (Abridged 1-hour CD)

———, *The Feel the Fear Guide to Lasting Love*. P.O. Box 5338, Santa Monica, CA 90409: Jeffers Press, 2005.

———, *I Can Handle It!: 50 Confidence-Building Stories to Empower Your Child*. P.O. Box 5338, Santa Monica, CA 90409: Jeffers Press, 2006. (For children ages 3–7)

———, *Life Is Huge!: Laughing, Loving, and Learning from It All*. P.O. Box 5338, Santa Monica, CA 90409: Jeffers Press, 2005.

———, *The Little Book of Confidence*. P.O. Box 5338, Santa Monica, CA 90409: Jeffers Press, 2005.

———, *The Little Book of Peace of Mind*. P.O. Box 5338, Santa Monica, CA 90409: Jeffers Press, 2005.

———, *Opening Our Hearts to Men*. New York: Fawcett Columbine, 1989.

Kanin, Garson, *It Takes a Long Time to Become Young*. New York: Doubleday and Company, 1978.

Keyes, Ken, *Handbook to Higher Consciousness*. P.O. Box 550, Marina Del Rey, CA 90291: Living Love Publications, 1980, 1983.

———, *How to Enjoy Your Life in Spite of It All*. P.O. Box 550, Marina Del Rey, CA 90291: Living Love Publications, 1980, 1983.

Kushner, Harold, *When All You've Ever Wanted Isn't Enough: The Search for a Life That Matters*. New York: Touchstone Books, Simon & Schuster, 1986, 2002.

Levine, Stephen, *A Gradual Awakening*. London: Rider and Company, 3 Fitzroy Square, nd.

May, Rollo, *Man's Search for Himself*. New York: W. W. Norton & Company, 2009.

Murphy, Joseph, *The Power of Your Subconscious Mind*. New York: Bantam Books, 1963, 1982.

Peale, Norman Vincent, *You Can If You Think You Can*. New York: Touchstone Books, Simon & Schuster, 1987.

Peck, M. Scott, *The Road Less Traveled: A New Psychology of Love, Traditional Values, and Spiritual Growth*, 25th anniversary ed. New York: Touchstone Books, Simon & Schuster, 2003.

Porter, Eleanor H., *Pollyanna*. New York: Farrar, Straus & Giroux, 1912.

Prather, Hugh, *There Is a Place Where You Are Not Alone*. New York: Doubleday Company, 1980.

Probstein, Bobbie, *Return to Center: The Flowering of Self-Trust.* Devorss & Co.; 1st Printing edition (September 1, 1985).

Rann, Michael, and Elizabeth Rann Arrott, *Shortcut to a Miracle: How to Change Your Consciousness and Transform Your Life.* DeVorss Publications; 2nd edition (January 1, 2005).

Rossman, Martin, M.D. *Healing Yourself: A Step-By-Step Program for Better Health Through Imagery.* New York: Walker and Company, 1987.

Sheehy, Gail, *Passages*, 20th anniversary ed. New York: Bantam Books, 2006.

———, *Pathfinders.* New York: William Morrow and Co., 1981.

Sher, Barbara, and Annie Gottlieb, *Wishcraft: How To Get What You Really Want.* New York: Ballantine Books, 2004.

Small, Jacquelyn, *Transformers: The Therapists of the Future.* Marina Del Rey, CA: DeVorss & Co., 1982, 1990.

White, Frank, *The Overview Effect: Space Exploration and Human Evolution.* Reston, VA: American Institute of Aeronautics & Astronautics, 1998.

Williams, Margery, *The Velveteen Rabbit.* New York: Doubleday & Co., 1922.

Williamson, Marianne, *The Gift of Change: Spiritual Guidance for Living Your Best Life.* San Francisco: HarperSanFrancisco, 2006.

Acknowledgments

Everybody needs a cheering squad rooting them on, and my cheerleaders are sensational! Nancy Miller and Christina Duffy at Ballantine Books; Martha Lawrence, whose belief in and appreciation of my work made the original edition *finally* happen 35 years ago; Dominick Abel, my agent, who never gave up and ultimately succeeded; Ruth Van Doren and the students at the New School for Social Research in New York City, who gave me a receptive environment to begin teaching my ideas about fear; Kathryn Welds, at the UCLA Extension, who welcomed my work in California; Diana von Welanetz Wentworth, the late Paul von Welanetz, and members of The Inside Edge, who stood on chairs and cheered every success; Roslyn Hayes, my teacher, who many years ago encouraged me to stretch as far as I could go; Sally Lefkowitz, an inspiration, who showed me what indomitable courage looks like; my loyal and caring friends, who applaud every step I take; my wonderful sister, Marcia, who is also my best friend, and my brother-in-law, Bruce, who does so much to help this world; my fabulous children, Gerry and Leslie, my stepchildren, Alice and Guy, and their partners, Michael, and Ashley, who add so much richness to my life; and, of course, my incredible husband, Mark, who walks beside me and comforts me every step of the way. I thank all of the above for playing such an important role in the quality of my life. Thank you! Thank you! Thank you!

About the Author

SUSAN JEFFERS, PhD, dubbed "the Queen of Self-Help" by the London *Times*, was the author of numerous bestsellers, published in more than one hundred countries and translated into dozens of languages. Her many books include *Feel the Fear . . . and Do It Anyway* (which has sold more than 15 million copies to date), *Feel the Fear . . . and Beyond, The Little Book of Confidence,* and *Life Is Huge!* Susan Jeffers died in 2012, but her passion, love, and insight continue to inform and inspire.